SHAMBHALA DRAGON EDITIONS

The dragon is an age-old symbol of the highest spiritual essence, embodying wisdom, strength, and the divine power of transformation. In this spirit, Shambhala Dragon Editions offers a treasury of readings in the sacred knowledge of Asia. In presenting the works of authors both ancient and modern, we seek to make these teachings accessible to lovers of wisdom everywhere.

Great Eastern Sun
The Wisdom of Shambhala

 CHÖGYAM TRUNGPA
Dorje Dradul of Mukpo

Edited by Carolyn Rose Gimian

SHAMBHALA • *Boston & London* • *2001*

SHAMBHALA PUBLICATIONS, INC.
Horticultural Hall
300 Massachusetts Avenue
Boston, Massachusetts 02115
www.shambhala.com

9 8 7 6 5 4 3 2 1

First Paperback Edition

Printed in the United States of America
⊗ This edition is printed on acid-free paper that meets the American National Standards Institute Z39.48 Standard.

Distributed in the United States by Random House, Inc., and in Canada by Random House of Canada Ltd

Library of Congress Cataloging-in-Publication Data

Trungpa, Chogyam, 1939–
Great eastern sun/Chögyam Trungpa (Dorje Dradul of Mukpo); ed. by Carolyn Rose Gimian.
p. cm.
ISBN 1-57062-293-0 (cloth)
ISBN 1-57062-818-1 (pbk.)
1. Spiritual life—Buddhism.   I. Gimian, Carolyn Rose.
II. Title.
BQ4302.T7824   1999   99-32291
294.3'444—dc21   CIP

TO GESAR OF LING

གེ་སར་ལ་བསྟོད་པ།

གོ་ཁྲབ་གསེར་གྱི་རི་མོས་མཛེས་པ་དང་།

རྟ་མཆོག་ཅ་ཚུན་སྣ་ཡིས་སྒྲུབས་པ་འདི།

དཔའ་བོ་དམག་དཔོན་ཁྱོད་ལ་གུས་པས་འབུལ།

མཐའ་ཡི་དམག་དཔུང་འཇོམས་པའི་ཕྱིན་ལས་མཛོད།

དཔའ་བོ་ཁྱོད་ཀྱི་གཟི་བརྗིད་དེ།

ཆར་སྤྲིན་དབུས་ཀྱི་གློག་ཞགས་འད།

འཇིགས་པ་དྲག་ཁྱོད་ཀྱི་འཆོམ་མདངས་དེ།

བཙོ་སྦྱེའི་སྣ་བ་ཚེས་པ་འད།

ཁྱོད་ཀྱི་མཐུ་སྟོབས་སྟོག་མེད་པ།

རྒྱ་སྨུག་གཟན་ལ་ཆས་པ་འད།

མང་པོའི་དཔུང་གིས་བསྐོར་བའི་དབུས།

ཁྱོད་ནི་གཡག་རྒོད་རྔམ་འད།

ཁྱོད་ཀྱི་དགྲ་བོ་རྒྱུར་པ་དེ།

རྩུ་སྦྲིན་ཁ་རུ་ཟིན་པ་འད།

ཕ་མེས་བརྒྱུད་པ་འཛིན་པའི་བུ་མ།

དཔའ་བོ་ཁྱོད་ཀྱིས་སྲུངས་སྐྱོབས་མཛོད།

To Gesar of Ling

Armor ornamented with gold designs,
Great horse adorned with sandalwood saddle:
These I offer you, great Warrior General—
Subjugate now the barbarian insurgents.

Your dignity, O Warrior,
Is like lightning in rain clouds.
Your smile, O Warrior,
Is like the full moon.
Your unconquerable power
Is like a tiger springing.
Surrounded by troops,
You are a wild yak.
Becoming your enemy
Is being caught by a crocodile:
O Warrior, protect me,
The ancestral heir.

Contents

Illustrations

Frontispiece   Photograph of the Dorje Dradul, taken when he was presenting "The Primordial Dot" in Boston, Massachusetts. © *1980 by Mary Lang.*

Title page, part titles, and cover stamp   The Great Eastern Sun. *Design by Chögyam Trungpa. Executed by Gina Stick.*

Page v   The Scorpion Seal, which is the seal of the Mukpo clan and of the Sakyong of Shambhala. It was previously used as the seal of the king of Dege, a kingdom in eastern Tibet. *Design by Chögyam Trungpa.*

Page vi   Tibetan script of "To Gesar of Ling" provided by the Nalanda Translation Committee.

Pages 28–29   Four photographs of the author executing a calligraphy of *lungta,* or windhorse. *Photographs by Andrea Roth. From the collection of the Shambhala Archives.*

Page 99   The Chinese and Tibetan characters for "imperial." The middle character, three horizontal lines joined by one vertical line, is the character for "king," described on p. 98. *Calligraphy by Chögyam Trungpa.*

Page 103   Photograph taken during a luncheon at the U.S. Capitol in 1980 in honor of His Holiness the Sixteenth Gyalwa Karmapa (see p. 102). Senator Charles Percy is being introduced to His Eminence Jamgon Kongtrul Rinpoche by the Karmapa. Chögyam Trungpa is shown to His Holiness's left, and the Tibetan translator is standing to His Holiness's right. The logo of the Karmapa can be seen on the banner behind them. *Photograph by U.S. Capitol Police. From the collection of the Shambhala Archives.*

Page 127   The logo of the Karmapa, showing two deer on either side of the wheel of dharma. The Tibetan inscription on the banner reads: "The

Seat of the Glorious Karmapa." *From the collection of the Shambhala Archives.*

Page 131 A statue of a *lohan,* or a disciple of the Buddha, shown in the posture of meditation. *From the collection of the British Museum.*

Page 143 His Holiness the Sixteenth Gyalwa Karmapa. *Photographer unknown. From the collection of the Shambhala Archives.*

Page 146 The Big No. *Calligraphy by Chögyam Trungpa. Reprinted from* First Thought Best Thought: 108 Poems, *by Chögyam Trungpa.*

Page 160 Tiger. *Photograph by Chögyam Trungpa.*

Pages 178, 179, 180, 181 The tiger, lion, garuda, and dragon. *Line drawings by Sherap Palden Beru.*

Page 197 Chögyam Trungpa teaching a dharma art program in Boulder, Colorado. Behind him can be seen his personal flag or standard, described on p. 197. To his right is the Shambhala flag, which he describes on p. 196. From top to bottom, the four stripes on the Shambhala flag are orange, white, red, and blue. *Photograph by Robert Del Tredici.*

Page 210 Chögyam Trungpa. *Photograph by Robert Del Tredici.*

Page 229 Chögyam Trungpa in a field behind the Balmoral Inn in Tatamagouche, Nova Scotia, 1979. *Photograph by James Gimian.*

Page 266 Tibetan script of the closing dedication provided by the Nalanda Translation Committee.

Endpapers The warrior's cry, Ki Ki So So. *Calligraphy by Chögyam Trungpa.*

List of Poems

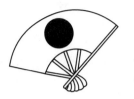# Foreword

ON BEHALF OF MY LATE HUSBAND, Chögyam Trungpa Rinpoche, and on behalf of the Mukpo family, I am very pleased to contribute a foreword to *Great Eastern Sun.* Trungpa Rinpoche, whose Shambhala title was Dorje Dradul of Mukpo, was a true example of a Shambhala person. Although he was raised in the strict monastic tradition of Tibet, he was very broad-minded. He was able to appreciate the fundamental sacredness of life and the lives of people from many different traditions. He not only followed the Buddhist path but also explored many different aspects of life, which included an interest in the visual arts, poetry, and so forth. He was able to see beyond his own tradition and to appreciate how the Shambhala principles might affect the lives of human beings with other religious affiliations or no particular religious affiliation at all. This is an example of what a compassionate person he was.

It would have been very important to my husband to know that these teachings, which he gave to his students during his lifetime, are now being presented in a book that can be available to many, many people. I hope that these principles can be brought onto whatever path people are traveling in their lives. It can help to enrich their lives and give them perspective. Some people may already naturally embody many of these principles. This book will help to give them a format and structure within which to live their lives.

In the Shambhala teachings, we often talk about the Great

Eastern Sun. The sun is always rising, which means that there is always the potential for human beings to discover their own goodness and the sacredness of the world. Therefore, we have entitled this book *Great Eastern Sun.* I hope that this book will help many people, including those who are already on the path of warriorship, to experience further Great Eastern Sun vision in their lives.

Trungpa Rinpoche himself lived his life by these principles and was therefore able to enrich the lives of others. I hope that people can take these principles to heart so that they, in turn, may be able to enrich the lives of those with whom they come in contact. You might say this is a bodhisattva approach to the Shambhala tradition. It was certainly my husband's approach to his entire life.

Diana Judith Mukpo
Providence, Rhode Island
October 17, 1998

 # Preface

THIS VOLUME IS A SEQUEL and a complement to *Shambhala: The Sacred Path of the Warrior*. The first volume was like a guidebook to Shambhala or a road map of the warrior's path. *Great Eastern Sun* is about transmission and about embodying and manifesting. In that sense, it is not about *then;* it is about *now.* There is a way in which this book attempts to directly convey or transmit wisdom. Although that is a rather difficult thing to do, it is couched within simplicity.

Great Eastern Sun is divided into a prologue and five parts—"Profound," "Brilliant," "Just," "Powerful," and "All-Victorious." The five divisions correspond to the five qualities of something called *absolute Ashé.* The word *Ashé* is not mentioned in the manuscript, but it will be found in the author's notes for the talks on which this book is based. (See author's notes, pp. 245–247.) In the Shambhala teachings, the Ashé principle represents the life force, or the basic energy that underlies and infuses all human life and activity. Readers can pursue further study of the Ashé principle through the Shambhala Training program.[1]

Although this book is structured in a deliberate order, it does not have to be read front to back. The material in the early chapters is more demanding logically; the later material is more atmospheric and sometimes more playful. In some sense, the structure

1. For information about Shambhala Training, see p. 249. For information about the history and structure of the Shambhala Training program and its relationship to the material in this book, please see the editor's afterword.

of the book is like a flower with petals unfolding. If you read it from beginning to end, you start at the outer petals and spiral in to an empty center. But you can also start in the middle or anywhere in between.

The material in the last two parts of the book, "Powerful" and "All-Victorious," is presented as a series of lectures that you, the reader, can attend. These chapters might be regarded as meditations. You may want to read them that way and see whether that approach works for you.

In presenting the Shambhala teachings to the Western world, Chögyam Trungpa not only charted new territory, but he also adopted a new name: Dorje Dradul of Mukpo. He signed the foreword to *Shambhala: The Sacred Path of the Warrior* with this name. *Mukpo* is his family name; *Dorje Dradul* means "The Adamantine, or Indestructible, Warrior." In this book, he is often referred to as the Dorje Dradul.[2]

New meditators and those who have never practiced meditation will, I think, find this book accessible. I hope that it will also be of interest to more seasoned practitioners. Many readers will be satisfied purely with what they gain from reading the book. Others may find the sitting practice of meditation to be a discipline they would like to pursue. There are many qualified meditation instructors and a number of organizations that offer an introduction to Buddhist and mindfulness meditation practice.[3] In the first book, *Shambhala*, detailed meditation instruction is pro-

2. In the Tibetan Buddhist tradition, it is not uncommon for both teachers and students to receive new names or titles in connection with religious vows they have taken or practices they are given. In keeping with the use of the author's Shambhala name in this book, I also have signed the editor's preface and afterword with both my Western and Shambhala names.

3. The practice of meditation and the teachings of Shambhala warriorship are offered by Shambhala Training in many locations in North America, South America, Europe, Australia, Africa, and parts of Asia. For information about Shambhala Training, see the resources section at the back of the book.

vided in the chapter entitled "Discovering Basic Goodness." In the present volume, a multilayered approach is taken to presenting the details of the sitting practice of meditation. Practice infuses the discussion in many chapters, but no separate instruction is provided.

Rather than defining a term thoroughly the first time it was used, I decided to let the definition and understanding of terms and concepts evolve throughout the book. The editor's afterword includes information on the sources used in the book and how the material was edited that may help to put this in context. I let terms be reintroduced many times. I felt this approach was in keeping with how the author originally presented this material. Like the mysterious primordial dot that pops up over and over again in this book, wisdom is always fresh. It is never redundant.

I hope that readers will, in this spirit, enjoy and explore the repetition of concepts and definitions in this book. Think of it, if you will, as though you were trying a dozen different varieties of apples over the course of the autumn. Whenever you bite into an apple, you experience the sameness, or the appleness, of the fruit as well as the particular flavor of the variety—Winesap, McIntosh, or Golden Delicious. Or you might approach this book like sipping fine single-malt whiskey or excellent green tea or enjoying a spicy curry. Each sip or each bite is the same, yet different. There is a deepening and blending of the flavors.

Music has a similar quality. The repetition, with variations, is obvious in many musical forms, from traditional music—such as the Indonesian gamelon, the Japanese gagaku, or the fiddle music of Scotland and Cape Breton—to the complexities of modern jazz. A fugue by Bach and a symphony by Beethoven also repeat their themes myriad times; songs have their choruses, which echo over and over.

Indeed, it may be helpful to think of the chapters in this book as a series of love songs. There is rarely any new information in a love song. What makes it interesting is *how* it expresses this most basic of human emotions. The life of Chögyam Trungpa Rinpoche was one long love song dedicated to sentient beings. It is a privilege to have been able to edit a few of the verses.

I hope you will enjoy these songs of basic goodness.

Dorje Yutri, Carolyn Rose Gimian

June 27, 1998
Halifax, Nova Scotia

· GREAT EASTERN SUN ·

 The Kingdom, the Cocoon,
the Great Eastern Sun

*The Shambhala training is based on developing gentleness and
genuineness so that we can help ourselves and develop tenderness
in our hearts. We no longer wrap ourselves in the sleeping bag of
our cocoon. We feel responsible for ourselves, and we feel good
taking responsibility. We also feel grateful that, as human beings,
we can actually work for others. It is about time that we did something to help the world. It is the right time, the right moment, for
this training to be introduced.*

DRIVEN BY SURVIVAL, hassled by the demands of life, we
live in a world completely thronged by holding on to our state of
existence, our livelihood, our jobs. People throughout this century
and for at least the last few thousand years have been trying to
solve our problems right and left. Throughout history, in fact,
great prophets, teachers, masters, gurus, yogins, saints of all kinds
have appeared and tried to solve the problems of life. Their message has been quite definite: "Try to be good. Be gentle to yourselves, to your neighbors, your parents, your relatives, your

spouse—to the whole world. If you are good to others, you will relieve their anxiety. Then you will have excellent neighbors, excellent relatives, an excellent wife, an excellent husband, an excellent world." That message has been presented a thousand times. Our lives are enriched by many sacred writings, including the ancient traditions of Taoism, Vedic texts, *sutras, tantras,* and *shastras*[1]—sacred texts of all kinds. Modern libraries and bookstores are filled with these attempts to reach us. People try so hard to help, even placing the Gideon Bible in hotel rooms.

Many of those teachers and saints belong to a theistic tradition. That is to say, they worship the one God, and they are monotheists, or they are presenting sacred messages from the multitheism of other traditions. On the other hand, Buddhism is a nontheistic spiritual discipline, which does not talk in terms of worship and does not regard the world as somebody's creation. According to the Buddhist teachings, there was no great artificer who fashioned the world. This world is created or produced and happens to be purely through our own existence. We exist; therefore, we have fashioned this particular world. Then there are entirely different schools of thought, supported by scientific discoveries, that say that everything is an evolutionary process. We have Darwinian theories of how, from a monkey or a fish, human beings came to exist.

There are many conflicting notions about the origins of existence. But whether it is according to theism, nontheism, or a scientific approach, there *is* this particular world—which is created and which we have. To theologians or scientists, it may be terribly important to figure out why we are here or how we came to be here. But from the point of view of Shambhala vision, the main concern is not *why* I am here or *why* you are here. *Why* you

1. Sutras are discourses by the Buddha; tantras are tantric Buddhist texts ascribed to the Buddha in his ultimate, or *dharmakaya,* form; and shastras are philosophical commentaries on the sutras.

happen to have a white shirt, a red shirt, long hair, or short hair is not the question. The real question is, Since we're here, how are we going to live from now onward? We may or may not have a long time to live. Impermanence is always there. Right now, you may cease to live. As you walk out of the room you're in right now, something may happen to you. You may face death. There are many eventualities of life or death. You may face physical problems, sicknesses of all kinds. You may be subject to cancer. Nonetheless, you have to live from now onward.

The basic point of the Shambhala teachings is to realize that there is no outside help to save you from the terror and the horror of life. The best doctor of the doctors and the best medicine of the medicines and the best technology of the technologies cannot save you from your life. The best consultants, the best bank loans, and the best insurance policies cannot save you. Eventually, you must realize that *you* have to do something rather than depending on technology, financial help, your smartness, or good thinking of any kind—none of which will save you. That may seem like the black truth, but it is the real truth. Often, in the Buddhist tradition, it is called the *vajra* truth, the diamond truth, the truth you cannot avoid or destroy. We cannot avoid our lives at all. We have to face our lives, young or old, rich or poor. Whatever happens, we cannot save ourselves from our lives at all. We have to face the eventual truth—not even the eventual truth but the *real* truth of our lives. We are here; therefore, we have to learn how to go forward with our lives.

This truth is what we call the wisdom of Shambhala. The introduction of such wisdom into North American culture is a historical landmark. However, my purpose is not to convert you to what I have to say. Rather, the more you understand, the more you will realize your own responsibility. So I am speaking to you not only from the point of view of the trumpeter but also from the point of view of the trumpetees. Rather than watching the trumpeter, what is important is to hear the trumpet music.

THE KINGDOM

According to tradition, the Kingdom of Shambhala was a kingdom in Central Asia where this wisdom was taught and an excellent society was created. In that society, the citizens' conduct and their behavior were based on having less anxiety. Essentially, anxiety comes from not facing the current situation you are in. The Kingdom of Shambhala and the citizens, the subjects, of Shambhala were able to face their reality. The Kingdom of Shambhala could be said to be a mythical kingdom or a real kingdom—to the extent that you believe in Atlantis or in heaven. It has been said that the kingdom was technologically advanced and that the citizens had tremendous intelligence. Spirituality was secularized, meaning that day-to-day living situations were handled properly. Life was not based on the worship of a deity or on vigorous religious practice, as such. Rather, that wonderful world of Shambhala was based on actually relating with your life, your body, your food, your household, your marital situations, your breath, your environment, your atmosphere.

According to the legends, the vision and the teachings of Shambhala were embodied in that Central Asian kingdom. If we go deeper, we could say that such a situation of sanity comes about because you connect with your own intelligence. Therefore, the Kingdom of Shambhala exists in your own heart right at this moment. You are a citizen of Shambhala and part of the Kingdom of Shambhala, without doubt. We are not trying to bring a myth into reality, which would be the wrong thing to do. Actually, I have even written a book to that effect, entitled *The Myth of Freedom*.[2] On the other hand, as human beings, we do possess the

2. Published in 1976 by Shambhala Publications.

sense faculties: we can see, we can hear, we can feel, we can think. Because of that, we can do something to bring about the Kingdom of Shambhala once again.

This time, it doesn't have to be a Central Asian kingdom. We aren't talking about going over there and digging up graves, digging up ruins, to find the remains of the truth of Shambhala. We are not talking about conducting an archaeological survey. On the other hand, we *might* be talking about some kind of archaeological survey, which is digging up our minds and our lives, which have been buried and covered with layers and layers of dirt. We have to rediscover something in our lives. Is it possible? It is very possible, extremely possible. How should we go about it?

From the very day of your birth, you have never really looked at yourself, your life, and your experiences in life. You have never really felt that you could create a good, decent world. Of course, you may have tried all sorts of things. You may have marched in the street in the name of the happiness of humanity, complained about the existing political system, written up new ideas and manifestos to prevent this and that—that pain, this pain, this confusion, that confusion. You may have been somewhat heroic, and you could say that you've tried your best. Nonetheless, have you found any real peace or rest? A real, dignified world has not been created.

Often, we are so angry and resentful, and we complain because of our aggression. Instead of short hair, we want long hair. Instead of long hair, we cut our hair short. Instead of a coat and tie, we want to wear jeans and a T-shirt. Instead of this, we do that. Instead of that, we do this. We try to find some easy way to gain the freedom and the vision of human society. Instead of eating peanut butter, we try eating brown rice. Instead of that, we try this; instead of this, we try that. That, this, this, that. We have tried so many things. Particularly in the United States, people have tried *so* hard to reestablish a good world. I appreciate that

5

integrity, which is quite relentless, in some sense, and pretty good.

However, the principle of the Shambhala training is that, instead of trying so hard to remove problems, you should reestablish or plant something positive. The point is that you don't have to take so many showers to remove the dirt. The real question is what clothes you put on after your shower and how you perfume and beautify your body. One shower is good enough; it makes you clean. Then, after that, if you continue to take showers, you become stark, too clean. There is certainly an absence of dirt, but what comes after that? There's no warmth, no dignity. Can't we do something more to bring reality and goodness into society?

THE COCOON

The point of the Shambhala training is to get out of the cocoon, which is the shyness and aggression in which we have wrapped ourselves. When we have more aggression, we feel more fortified. We feel good, because we have more to talk about. We feel that we are the greatest author of the complaint. We write poetry about it. We express ourselves through it. Instead of constantly complaining, can't we do something positive to help this world? The more we complain, the more concrete slabs will be put on the earth. The less we complain, the more possibilities there will be of tilling the land and sowing seeds. We should feel that we can do something positive for the world instead of covering it with our aggression and complaints.

The approach of the Shambhala training is to do something very concrete, very basic, very definite, and to begin at the beginning. In the Shambhala tradition, we talk about being a warrior. I would like to make it clear that a warrior, in this case, is not someone who wages war. A Shambhala warrior is someone who is brave enough not to give in to the aggression and contradictions that exist in society. A warrior, or *pawo* in Tibetan, is a brave person, a genuine person who is able to step out of the cocoon— that very comfortable cocoon that he or she is trying to sleep in.

If you are in your cocoon, occasionally you shout your complaints, such as: "Leave me alone!" "Bug off." "I want to be who I am." Your cocoon is fabricated out of tremendous aggression, which comes from fighting against your environment, your parental upbringing, your educational upbringing, your upbringing of all kinds. You don't really have to fight with your cocoon. You can raise your head and just take a *little* peek out of the cocoon. Sometimes, when you first peek your head out, you find the air a bit too fresh and cold. But still, it is good. It is the best fresh air of spring or autumn or, for that matter, the best fresh air of winter or summer. So when you stick your neck out of the cocoon for the first time, you like it in spite of the discomfort of the environment. You find that it's delightful. Then, having peeked out, you become brave enough to climb out of the cocoon. You sit on your cocoon and look around at your world. You stretch your arms, and you begin to develop your head and shoulders. The environment is friendly. It is called "planet earth." Or it is called "Boston" or "New York City." It is your world.

Your neck and your hips are not all that stiff, so you can turn and look around. The environment is not as bad as you thought. Still sitting on the cocoon, you raise yourself up a little further. Then you kneel, and finally you stand up on your cocoon. As you look around, you begin to realize that the cocoon is no longer useful. You don't have to buy the advertisers' logic that, if you don't have insulation in your house, you're going to die. You don't really need the insulation of your cocoon. It's just a little cast that's been put on you by your own collective imaginary paranoia and confusion, which didn't want to relate with the world outside.

Then, you extend one leg, rather tentatively, to touch the ground around the cocoon. Traditionally, the right leg goes first.

You wonder where your foot is going to land. You've never touched the soles of your feet before on the soil of this planet earth. When you first touch the earth, you find it's very rough. It's made out of earth, dirt. But soon you discover the intelligence that will allow you to *walk* on the earth, and you begin to think the process might be workable. You realize that you inherited this family heirloom, called "planet earth," a long time ago.

You sigh with relief, maybe a medium sigh, extend your left foot, and touch the ground on the other side of the cocoon. The second time you touch the ground, to your surprise you find that the earth is kind and gentle and much less rough. You begin to feel gentleness and affection and softness. You feel that you might even fall in love on your planet earth. You *can* fall in love. You feel real passion, which is very positive.

At that point, you decide to leave your old beloved cocoon behind and to stand up without touching the cocoon at all. So you stand on your two feet, and you take a walk outside of the cocoon. Each step is rough and soft, rough and soft: rough because the exploration is still a challenge and soft because you don't find anything trying to kill you or eat you up at all. You don't have to defend yourself or fight any unexpected attackers or wild beasts. The world around you is so fine and beautiful that you know that you can raise yourself up as a warrior, a powerful person. You begin to feel that the world is absolutely workable, not even merely workable, but *wonderful.* To your surprise, you find that lots of others around you are also leaving their cocoons. You find hosts of ex-cocooners all over the place.

As ex-cocooners, we feel that we can be dignified and wonderful people. We do not have to reject anything at all. As we step out of our cocoons, we find goodness and gratefulness taking place in us all the time. As we stand on the earth, we find that the world is not particularly depressed. On the other hand, there is need for tremendous hard work. As we stand up and walk around, having finally got out of our own cocoons, we see that there are hundreds of thousands of others who are still half breathing in their cocoons. So we feel very touched and sad, extremely sad.

From the dictionary's point of view, *sadness* has negative connotations. If you feel sad, you feel unfortunate or bad. Or you are sad because you don't have enough money or you don't have any security. But from the Shambhala point of view, sadness is also inspiring. You feel sad and empty-hearted, but you also feel something positive, because this sadness involves appreciation of others. You would like to tell those who are still stuck in their cocoons that, if they got out of the cocoon, they would also feel that genuine sadness. That empty-heartedness is the principle of the broken-hearted warrior. As an ex-cocooner, you feel it is wonderful that people of the past have gotten out of their cocoons. You wish that you could tell the cocooners the story of the warriors of the Great Eastern Sun and the story of the Kingdom of Shambhala. All the warriors of the past had to leave their cocoons. You wish you could let the cocooners know that. You would like to tell them that they are not alone. There are hundreds of thousands of others who have made this journey.

Once you develop this quality of sadness, you also develop a quality of dignity or positive arrogance within yourself, which is quite different from the usual negative arrogance. You can manifest yourself with dignity to show the degraded world that trying to avoid death by sleeping in a cocoon is not the way. The degraded world, in which people are sleeping in their cocoons trying to avoid the pain of death, is called the setting-sun world. In that world, people are looking for the sunset as a sign that there will be a peaceful night ahead. But that night is never peaceful: it is always pitch-dark. Those who arise from the cocoon are called the people of the Great Eastern Sun. They are not blinded by opening their eyes, and they are not embarrassed about developing head and shoulders and stepping out of their cocoons. Such people begin to breathe the fresh morning air. They experience brilliance, which is constant and beautiful.

In the sitting practice of meditation, which is part of the Shambhala training, we stress the importance of good posture. Posture is important, not just in sitting practice, but in whatever you do. Whether you are talking to a client or talking to your mate, whether you're talking to your pets or talking to yourself—which does sometimes happen—having a good posture of head and shoulders is an expression that you've stepped out of your cocoon. One of the reasons that people sing in the shower is that the water showering down on you forces you to stand up and have good head and shoulders. You begin to feel cleaned out, so you begin to sing or hum. This is not a myth; it's true. When you have water falling on your shoulders, your head, and your face, there's a sense that you're relating with heaven.

HELPING OTHERS

The Shambhala training is based on developing gentleness and genuineness so that we can help ourselves and develop tenderness in our hearts. We no longer wrap ourselves in the sleeping bag of our cocoon. We feel responsible for ourselves, and we feel good taking responsibility. We also feel grateful that, as human beings, we can actually work for others. It is about time that we did something to help the world. It is the right time, the right moment, for this training to be introduced.

The fixation of ego is manifested in the words *I am.* Then there is the conclusion: "I am . . . happy" or "I am . . . sad." There is the first thought (I) and the second thought (am), and finally the third thought is the conclusion. "I am *happy,*" "I am *sad,*" "I feel *miserable,*" "I feel *good*"—whatever the thought may be. The Shambhala idea of responsibility is to drop *am.* Just say, "I happy," "I sad." I know there's a bit of a linguistic problem here, but I hope that you can understand what I'm saying. The point is to be responsible to others, without self-confirmation.

To put it slightly differently, suppose your name is Sandy. There is "Sandy," and there is the "world." You don't need a verb between them as confirmation. Just be kind to others. Sandy should be genuine. When she is the real, genuine Sandy, she can help others a lot. She may not have any training in first aid, but Sandy can put a Band-Aid on someone's finger. Sandy is no longer afraid to help, and she is very kind and on the spot. When you begin to help others, you have raised your head and shoulders, and you're stepping out of your cocoon. The point of the Shambhala training is not to produce fake people. The point is to become a real person who can help others.

Being in the cocoon is almost like being a child in the womb, a child who doesn't particularly want to come out. Even after you're born, you aren't happy about being toilet-trained. You would prefer to stay in your nappies, your diapers. You like to have something wrapped around your bottom all the time. But eventually, your diapers are taken away. You have no choice. You have been born, and you've been toilet-trained; you can't stay forever in your diapers. In fact, you might feel quite free, no longer having a diaper wrapped around your bum. You can move around quite freely. You might eventually feel quite good about being free from the tyranny that parenthood and home life impose.

Still, we don't *really* want to develop discipline. So we begin to create this little thingy, this little cocoon. We get wrapped up in all sorts of things. When we're in the cocoon, we don't want to sit upright and eat with good table manners. We don't really want to dress elegantly, and we don't want to conform to any discipline that requires even three minutes of silence. That's partly because of being raised in North America, where everything is built for children to entertain themselves. Entertainment is even the basis for education. If you can raise your own children outside of the cocoon, you will raise lots of bodhisattva children, children who are real and face facts and are actually able to relate with reality properly. I have done that myself with my own children, and it seems to have worked out.

As decent human beings, we face the facts of reality. Whether we are in the middle of a snowstorm or a rainstorm, whether there is family chaos, whatever problems there may be, we are willing to work them out. Looking into those situations is no longer regarded as a hassle, but it is regarded as our duty. Although helping others has been preached quite a lot, we don't really believe we can do it. The traditional American expression, as I've heard it, is that we don't want to get our fingers dirty. That, in a nutshell, is why we want to stay in the cocoon: we don't want to get our fingers dirty. But we must do something about this world, so that the world can develop into a nonaggressive society where people can wake themselves up. Helping others is one of the biggest challenges.

I appreciate your inquisitiveness, your sense of humor, and your relaxation. Please try to elegantize yourselves and step out of the cocoon. The basic point is to become very genuine within yourselves. This means being free from the plastic world, if such a thing is possible. Also, please don't hurt others. If you can't do that, at least treat yourself better and don't punish yourself by sleeping in your cocoon. Finally, please try to work with people and be helpful to them. A fantastically large number of people need help. *Please* try to help them, for goodness sake, for heaven and earth. Don't just collect Oriental wisdoms one after the other. Don't just sit on an empty *zafu,* an empty meditation cushion. But go out and try to help others, if you can. That is the main point.

We have to do something. We've *got* to do something. As we read in the newspapers and see on television, the world is deteriorating, one thing after the other, every hour, every minute, and nobody is helping very much. Your help doesn't have to be a big deal. To begin with, just work with your friends and work with yourself at the same time. It is about time that we became responsible for this world. It will pay for itself.

PART ONE

PROFOUND

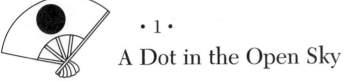

· 1 ·

A Dot in the Open Sky

Our theme here is trust. To begin with, the notion of trust is being without suspicion. That is the idea of trust from the dictionary's point of view. When you trust somebody, you're not suspicious of them at all. Trust without suspicion strangely comes from nowhere, but we are not talking about a mystical experience. When you trust without suspicion, what are you left with? When there's no suspicion, what is your trust in anyway? You are right on the dot. Trust without suspicion.

WE ARE WORTHY TO LIVE IN THIS WORLD. The Shambhala journey is a process of learning to appreciate and understand this worthiness. The training is based on the discipline of uplifting and civilizing ourselves, which is partly a reflection of the *buddhadharma*, the teachings of the Buddha. Buddhism provides an idea of how to handle ourselves: body, mind, speech, and livelihood all together. The Shambhala training is also a response to suffering and pain, the misery, terror, and horror that have developed throughout what is known as the setting-sun world: a world based on the fear of death, fear of oneself, and fear of others—a world that comes with lots of warnings.

We have no idea how to actually live and lead our lives in today's society. How can we be decent human beings, dignified human beings, awake human beings? How can we conduct ourselves properly in this society, without laying trips on others or ourselves? How can we treat our children better, our husbands better, our wives better? How can we relate with our business partners better, our bosses better, our employees better? In response to those questions, the Shambhala idea of warriorship is quite practical. It is learning how to conduct our lives according to what is known as the Great Eastern Sun vision. The vision of the Great Eastern Sun is perpetually looking ahead, looking forward. Basically speaking, it is impossible not to go forward. You are always getting older—or younger. You can't hold off your death. Beyond that, every day you learn something new. You can't deny that. You may not have a particularly extraordinary vision every day. You may not make a billion dollars in a day—although sometimes such things come up as well! Nevertheless, there is always some kind of forward motion. There is no problem with going forward, but there is a difference between going forward and speeding recklessly. When you go forward, you go step-by-step. Recklessness is pushing yourself to do more than you can, or it is the result of impatience and being fearful. Rather than taking the time to prepare a nice meal, you eat bad fast food and get sick from it. Just go ahead. Just do it. Rebel—against something or other. There is no dignity.

Dignity is having consideration for others and being gentle to yourself and others. With gentleness, you go forward without recklessness, and the result is that you avoid any accidents. One analogy for that is riding a horse. If you have a good seat on the horse, good posture, and proper control of the reins, then as the horse moves forward, you and the horse are synchronized, so that

18

the horse never bucks and throws you off. Your gait is fantastic. Walk, and everything is controlled. You sit in the saddle as if you were on a throne. You have a good relationship with the horse, and your riding is good. In the Shambhala world, when mind and body are synchronized, you never mess up anybody else's situation. Recklessness is destroying other people's state of mind as well as your own. With Great Eastern Sun vision, that is out of the question. So the Shambhala training is learning how to be gentle to ourselves and others and learning why that *works* better. This particular training process educates us to become very decent human beings so that we can work with domestic situations and with our emotional life properly. We can synchronize our mind and body together, and without resentment or aggression, with enormous gentleness, we treat ourselves so well. In that way, we celebrate life properly.

The Shambhala path involves individual training. You might say that there is no new message here and that you've heard these things before, which may be true. There is no new message, particularly, or new trick. But the point here is to *actualize*. That in itself is a new message—which might be a new trick as well. People may give you lots of advice, trying to help you be good. They keep saying, "How're you doing? Take it easy. Don't worry. Everything's going to be OK." But nobody knows *how* to make that so. Can you really take it easy? Are you really going to be OK? This training presents how to do it. It presents the real heart of the matter. By joining the basic Buddhist-oriented practice of sitting meditation with the appreciation of our lives, there is no discrepancy between dealing with ourselves and dealing with others at all.

Our theme here is trust. To begin with, the notion of trust is being *without suspicion*. That is the idea of trust from the dictionary's point of view. When you trust somebody, you're not suspicious of them at all. Trust *without suspicion* strangely comes from nowhere, but we are not talking about a mystical experience. When you trust without suspicion, what are you left with? When there's no suspicion, what is your trust *in* anyway? You are right on the dot. Trust without suspicion.

When you are suspicious of someone or something, then you study that person or situation, and you say to yourself, "Suppose this happens. Then that might happen. If that happens, then this might happen." You imagine possible scenarios, you build up your logical conclusions, and you create a plan to rid yourself of any potential danger—which prevents any form of trust. In our case, the idea of trust without suspicion involves giving up any possibilities of a warning system for danger at all. In the Shambhala context, we are talking about unconditional trust. Unconditional trust means, first of all, that your own situation is trustworthy. You are as you are. Karen Doe is a good Karen Doe. Joe Schmidt is a good Joe Schmidt, a trustworthy Joe Schmidt. You trust in your existence and in your training. You *are* trustworthy; therefore, you can work with others. You don't have to pollute the world or give in to any indulgence at all.

Unconditional trust: we are capable of being good, kind, gentle, and loving, either to ourselves or to others. Why so? Because we have a gap somewhere in our state of mind. You might be the most cruel and mean person in history—a terrible person—but you are capable of falling in love. There is that possibility—not even possibility, but there *is* that actuality already. We are capable of being kind, loving, and gentle. In the English language, usually those words—*kind, loving, gentle*—refer purely to ethics or to our actions alone. But here those terms refer to our fundamental state of mind. With the state of mind of kindness and gentleness, we are capable of falling in love; we are capable of being gentle; we are capable of shaking hands with someone and saying, "Hello. How are you today?" That little capability—how little it may be! But we *have* something there. We are not complete monsters. We *do* occasionally smile. We look at someone, and we feel good. It may be only for a short period, but we have something in ourselves, and if we cultivate that experience, that dot of goodness, that spot, then we find that we have a dot in the open sky.

That dot was not produced by anybody. It wasn't part of our education or our upbringing or our relationship with our family or our love affairs. It's not part of our love of good food or good clothing. But that very soft spot, that tinge of something, is a dot in the sky. The dot is always there; it's primordial. We didn't even inherit it. *Inherited* means that something is handed down by generations. But in this case, we simply *have* it. Therefore, it is called the primordial, unconditional dot. That dot exists in a *big* sky. Often, we think it is a small sky, and we think the dot is just a mishap of some kind. We think it's an accident that we have that soft spot. *It* didn't mean it. We can just cover it up and forget it altogether. But there is a good dot in the sky, and that very dot is primordial, unconditioned basic goodness.

The dot is also the *source* of basic goodness, its fuse or starting point. Out of that primordial experience, we begin to realize basic goodness. To begin with, whenever there is a dot, it is unconditional. You can't say whether it is bad or good, but it is so. Then out of that dot of unconditional goodness comes the second level of basic goodness, which is the state of mind that is *willing*, always willing, to do things. To begin with, you are willing to acknowledge basic goodness. The obstacles to willingness are laziness and selfishness, which are a temporary patchwork that covers up the dot. But fundamentally, underneath that, there is always willingness. You are willing to sacrifice yourself for somebody else. On a certain day, you might feel terribly uptight. Then you feel your dot. After that, you might end up saying to somebody, "Hello. How are you?"

That willingness is almost an automatic thing, not something that you have to crank up, but a basic human instinct that happens

21

all the time. Habitual patterns of neurosis don't provide any real obstacles to it. The pattern of habitual neurosis is to hold back, be uptight, and maintain your "thingy." But such neurosis doesn't reach very far fundamentally at all, because willingness is a natural reflex. You're driving with a friend in the middle of the night, and you look out the window of the car and see a shooting star. You think that your friend hasn't seen it, so without thinking, without hesitation, you say, "Did you see *that*?" Willingness and the dot take place at virtually the same time. The dot is the inspiration. It provides a connection, an inspiration, to being fundamentally good. Boing! You feel that you are you. Therefore, you can treat other people as you treat yourself. The dot is first thought. There's always the number zero. That's the dot. Otherwise, the rest of the numbers can't happen. That's it: the beginning of the beginning.

When you have children, you have to appreciate yourself as a mother or father and identify with being a parent. You are you, and you are a real parent, a good parent. Then you can relate with your children properly. It's quite organic. Plants, trees, and vegetables treat us that way. First they grow, and then they yield their fruit or themselves to be eaten. We cook them and make a good meal out of them. But human beings are usually more fishy: we haven't been able to yield to the fullest extent. We could actually become more like plants. First, just *be*—be a person—and then be a person to others. In that way, we can serve others and correct other people's problems. That kind of wanting to share, wanting to work with others, is always there.

When you are willing to relate with a situation, there is lots of room to express yourself, thoroughly and fully. When you realize that you are not frozen or completely hardened at all, that makes you more soft, vulnerable, and gentle. So when you have experienced the dot and the willingness, then gentleness arises. The opposite of gentleness is doubt and lack of humor. Doubt takes a lot of forms. One of them is the fear that you'll hurt yourself by going forward too much. That is doubt in the Great Eastern Sun principle, thinking that if you go forward, you might get hurt. Another form of doubt is feeling that you have fundamentally misunderstood your life. You feel that you are constantly making some kind of general mistake. You feel confused and condemned. In the middle of the night, if you have insomnia, you wonder when the sun is going to shine. Your clock seems to be made of rubber: time stretches longer and longer, and the sun never shines. There could be many levels of doubt, but all of those are manifested in a long face without a smile.

Freedom from doubt is connected with humor, joy, and celebration. You trust the situation; therefore, you can afford to smile. You don't have to hold back or be uptight. In that way, trust brings gentleness, doubtlessness, and relaxation. You experience the open sky.

This is all under the heading of that fundamental or larger vision of trust. We are not talking about a little trust, here and there, but we are talking about a big trust. In that connection, I would also like to talk about trusting yourself in the practice of meditation. The discipline of meditation is designed so that everybody can become a good person. Everybody should have a regal existence. When you sit on your meditation cushion, don't hesitate: try to be regal. Synchronize mind and body and try to have good physical posture. In meditation, you should keep everything very simple. Work with everything simply and directly, keep a good posture, follow the breath, and then project your mind. Work with your breath. Go along with the breath, which is simple and ordinary. Then include your discursive thoughts in your practice, and continually go back to your breath. At the same time, try to drive yourself. Be there as much as you can—on the spot. The sitting practice is not all that arduous. Just try to relate with the earthiness and ordinariness of it.

We are talking not only about the attainment of enlightenment but about becoming good human beings and good citizens. Goodness comes from your mind. The mind relates with your body, and the body relates with your circulation, breath, posture, and temperature. Try to combine all those things together. Try to have a very good, solid sitting practice. Be on the spot as much as you can. Breath goes out and dissolves. Another breath goes out. With good head and shoulders, open chest, you sit like a warrior. A sense of individual dignity takes place.

If you have any doubt about whether you're doing the meditation practice right or wrong, it doesn't matter all that much. The main point is to have honesty within yourself. Just do what you think is best. That is called self-truth. If truth is understood by oneself, then you cannot be persecuted at all, karmically or any other way. You're doing your best, so what can go wrong? Cheer up and have a good time. You have your dot already, whether you like it or not, so you're bound to do good. That is the saving grace.

1111 PEARL STREET
Off Beat

In the clear atmosphere,
A dot occurred.
Passion tinged that dot vermilion red,
Shaded with depression pink.
How beautiful to be in the realm of nonexistence:
When you dissolve, the dot dissolves;
When you open up, clear space opens.
Let us dissolve in the realm of passion,
Which is feared by the theologians and lawmakers.
Pluck, pluck, pluck, pluck the wild flower.
It is not so much of orgasm,
But it is a simple gesture,
To realize fresh mountain air that includes the innocence
    of a wild flower.
Come, come, D.I.R., you could join us.
The freshness is not a threat, not a burden;
It is a most affectionate gesture—
That a city could dissolve in love of the wildness of country
    flowers.
No duty, no sacrifice, no trap;
The world is full of trustworthy openness.
Let us celebrate in the cool joy
The turquoise blue
Morning dew
Sunny laughter
Humid home:
Images of love are so good and brilliant.

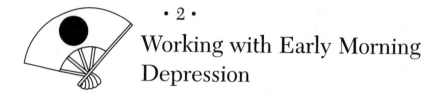

· 2 ·
Working with Early Morning Depression

In the Shambhala tradition, we talk about how fearlessness comes out of the realization of fear. Similarly, when you experience morning depression, it is possible to cheer up. That situation is genuine and quite workable. From morning depression and its terror, we can step right into basic goodness. We learn to reject the terror of morning depression and to step into morning basic goodness, right on the spot.

THE WHOLE SHAMBHALA TRAINING PROCESS is connected with how to *manifest,* so that people can do things without deception. We have to start right at the beginning, take it from the top, so to speak, or from the ground up. You are invited to join us. As they say, charity begins at home.

There are many international problems, and throughout the world, chaos is taking place all the time—which is obviously far from the expression of enlightened society. In the past, various disciplines or faiths—such as Christianity, Judaism, Hinduism, Islam, Buddhism—had great dignity. There were extraordinarily sane people among the ancients who worked to make the world worthwhile and passed down their wisdom generation by generation. But there has been a problem of corruption. The world has been seduced by physical materialism as well as by psychological materialism, let alone spiritual materialism! The world is beginning to turn sour. Our measures may be small at this point, but we're trying to sweeten the world up. In the long run, we want to offer something beyond a token. We want to make a real contribution to the development of enlightened society. That begins right here.

There's always the primordial dot—that spark of goodness that exists even before you think. We are worthy of that. Everybody possesses that unconditioned possibility of cheerfulness, which is not connected purely with either pain or pleasure. You have an inclination: in the flash of one second, you feel what needs to be done. It is not a product of your education; it is not scientific or logical; you simply pick up on the message. And then you act: you just do it. That basic human quality of suddenly opening up is the best part of human instinct. You know what to do right away, on the spot—which is fantastic. That is what we call the dot, or basic goodness and unconditional instinct. When you have an instinct of the real instinct, you don't think: you just feel, on the spot. Basic trust is knowing that there is such a thing as that spark of basic goodness. Although you might be in the worst of the worst shape, still that goodness does exist.

From trust comes renunciation. *Renunciation* is traditionally a term for rejecting or giving something up. But in the Shambhalian use of the term, renunciation is not giving up something like alcohol or cigarettes or sex. Renunciation here is connected with *knowing*—or with a general sense of discrimination. *Discrimination,* from the dictionary's point of view, might mean throwing away something bad and picking up on something good. But *dis-*

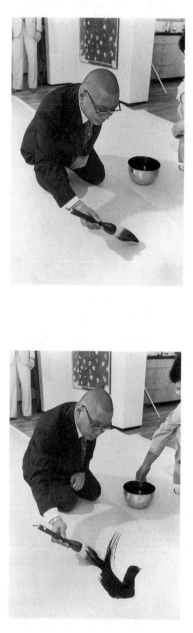

crimination in the Shambhala world means clear seeing or clear thinking. What it boils down to is precision. Anything that is not precise is rejected. When we talk about a Shambhala style of livelihood or about synchronizing mind and body together, those points are connected with how to *be there*, how to be precise. By means of discipline and training, mind and body can be well groomed. Renunciation doesn't mean that you develop one-up-manship and criticize or reject others who haven't practiced. We simply take pride in our own life, our own existence, our sparkiness, brilliance, fearlessness, and warriorship. The joy of basic goodness is the key to that.

Having experienced that first dot, what comes next? What comes next is the *appreciation* of that first good thought, which is called the stroke. Coming out of the first dot is the brushwork, just as when you touch an actual brush and ink to paper. First, you touch the ground, the canvas or the paper, and then you create a stroke, a calligraphy or a painting. The stroke of goodness is connected with second thought. From the first thought, the dot, you extend the second thought, which arises from gentleness. You are not trying to fight with your world or to destroy anything, nor are you trying to gain anything personally. There is just the first flash, and then there is the sense of continuing that.

If you're true to yourself, as you draw out your stroke, you begin to realize what is good for you and what is bad for you. We're talking here about working further with our basic instinct as human beings rather than operating on a purely materialistic, scientific, or analytical level. However, we're not saying that human beings are animals who need to be made into human beings. That is not the idea of enlightened society. Rather, we're saying that you have yourself, your existence as a human being, and you can work with what you have. You can develop that sense of basic instinct, which is pure and absolutely immaculate. There will be obstacles—questions, criticisms, moral and ethical choices—but you can overcome the ob-

29

stacles by acting as a true human being, which is bound to be good. You are a dignified and capable person already. So why don't you do it? That's the idea.

The starting point, that first delight, the dot, could be anything in your experience. Suppose you are very thirsty, and you are presented with a glass of ice water. The first thought, or the dot, occurs when you hold the glass of ice water and you are about to drink, knowing that it is the real thing and that it will quench your thirst. Then, holding the glass in your hand, you bring your arm close to your mouth, you bend your neck, you raise the glass, and you begin to drink. Having had the idea, the connection, the first delight, the stroke is that you proceed with the appreciation of that basic goodness. Strangely enough, when you are very thirsty, while you are drinking a glass of water, your mind is almost completely without anxiety at all. You can try this yourself. While you're drinking a glass of water, you have no thoughts. You are purely synchronizing your mind and body together in drinking that nice, cool glass of water. That is the concept of the stroke.

The stroke is the smoothness that comes along with the appreciation of basic goodness. With anything in life, it works that way. The closest analogy I can think of at this point is the general basic goodness of drinking a glass of ice water. It might be the wrong season to discuss this, but you can imagine it, I'm sure. You have an idea, and then you proceed with it. When you go along with that process, there is nonthought—almost. The joy of goodness. That goodness means that you are not creating pain for others and you are not indulging yourself either.

Then we have the second part of renunciation, which might be slightly painful. It is a sense of being put off, joined together with a sense of sadness, toward what is known as the setting-sun world. In that world, there is no perpetual vision, no forward vision, and your vision is purely connected with death and with things ending. Everything is getting dark. Dark pitch-blackness is about to come along, and we can't even see each other in this pitch-darkness without sunshine. The setting sun is the notion of eternal depression. When you feel depressed, when you feel bad, it is sometimes for no reason at all. You wake up in the morning and feel hopeless, terrible. We may use our experiences to justify that feeling: I feel bad—because I don't have any money. I feel bad—because I don't have any friends. I feel bad—because something has gone wrong in my life. I feel bad—because I'm not up to the challenge of firing someone at work this afternoon. I feel bad—because my husband left me.

In fact, our early morning depression is not all that logical. It is the curse of the setting sun. Out of nowhere, you just don't feel so good. *Then* you come up with all kinds of logical explanations for why you are depressed. There is a feeling of death. For some people, that feeling is completely extended, further and further, leading to a suicidal mentality. The other approach is to replace or repress your depression by doing something very crazy or reckless. Everybody knows this fundamental depression.

We do all sorts of things to avoid depression: waiting for the arrival of the newspaper at our house in the morning; even watching *Sesame Street* with our children—or without our children. There are lots of aids to forget depression, and billions and billions of dollars are spent on those attempts to cheer up. In England, many people like to bring their tea to their bath, and they drink their tea and take a long bath. Many of us use magazines and food to cheer ourselves up. We call up a friend to make a lunch appointment so that our early morning depression can be relieved by having a chat with somebody and making a lunch date. But what about the evening? That hasn't been worked out yet!

You may want to plan ahead, knowing that you might have this depression every morning, every day. So you plan a holiday to go skiing, surfing, or swimming. You need to take some time off— from what, one never knows, but you plan to take time off, telling yourself that you'll have a good time here and there. You try to keep things organized even a few days ahead so that you can avoid your early morning depression. In three weeks, you're going to go here and here and here, and you're going to do this and this and this. You tell yourself that you shouldn't be depressed, because you can look forward to what you've planned. You can keep on doing that almost indefinitely.

That is the basic idea of the setting sun. Hotels are built to promote that and airlines to accommodate it. Everything works toward helping us forget our early morning depression. From the point of view of basic goodness, we are capable of generating our own dignity and goodness. So yielding to that setting-sun mentality seems pathetic and quite sad, very sad. It is only going to get sadder as time goes on, unless we do something about it. No doubt the modern world will come up with further and more sophisticated aids to forget any reality of depression at all and to provide a million percent setting-sun world. The alternative is that, having experienced the joy of basic goodness and the sadness of the setting-sun world, we develop real renunciation, which is knowing what to accept and what to reject.

At this point, we need to understand another reference point, which is our habitual tendencies. I would like to make it quite clear that I am *not* saying that you're stuck with your habitual tendencies. When you are nice to a dog, it will always waggle its tail. In the same way, if you say hello to a person, he or she will automatically smile. But those are just reflexes rather than habitual tendencies. The habitual tendencies that I'm talking about here are the medium-level tendencies, which definitely can be overcome. Whether it is according to the wisdom of the Buddha or whether it is according to the wisdom of Shambhala, we are basically good. We possess what is known as basic goodness. Then we develop an overlay of unnecessary tricks and occupations. We develop little tricks to shield ourselves from being embarrassed or from feeling too painful or naked. Those are habitual tendencies, but they are not fundamental. They are simply temporary habitual tendencies. It's as though you had a building with nice, white, smooth plaster walls. If you can't stand the plain white walls, you might decide to put colorful wallpaper on top of them to cheer yourself up. The habitual tendencies we're talking about here are like the wallpaper that you put on but that can be taken off. The paper doesn't go all the way through the wall; it's not that deeply ingrained. It's a veneer of some kind, called habitual tendencies—which have to be renounced, definitely.

Seeing the basic goodness in oneself and seeing the sadness of the setting-sun possibilities, one is willing to make some kind of sacrifice. We can take off the wallpaper, take off the veneer. The negative aspect of renunciation, so to speak, is what you reject or avoid. In this case, you are rejecting self-indulgence, purely pleasing yourself. If you reject that, you have a clean white plaster wall. What you accept, on the positive side, is the development of genuine warriorship. In the Shambhala tradition, we talk about how fearlessness comes out of the realization of fear. Similarly, when you experience morning depression, it is possible to cheer up. That situation is genuine and quite workable. From morning depression and its terror, we can step right into basic goodness. We learn to reject the terror of morning depression and to step into morning basic goodness, right on the spot.

The result is that you have a better relationship with your mate, your kitchen is cleaner, your daily schedule is accomplished on time—all because you don't have a tremendous struggle, even on the smallest, most mundane level. You might think this is purely a Dear Abby concept of happiness, but in fact we're talking about developing enlightened society. Enlightened society comes from the kitchen sink level, from the bedroom level. Otherwise, there's no enlightened society, and everything is purely a hoax. So genuine renunciation is knowing what to accept and what to reject and how to step out and appreciate depression as a stair-case. When you put your foot on the first step of this very feeble staircase, you wonder whether it is going to hold you. You might fall. But as you take the third, fourth, and fifth steps, you realize that, although it's wobbly, it is going to carry you upstairs. And the journey is worthwhile.

In this way, you can begin to work with your early morning depression. First you wonder whether you can work with it or not, but once you take at least five steps, or have five thoughts—which is very fast; naturally, we think very fast for our own secur-ity—then you find that your early morning depression is fine. You can work with it, you can walk on it, and it will lead you into basic goodness. Walking on the staircase of your early morning depression is the concept of the stroke. The dot is taking the first step on the staircase, which is wobbly. One wonders . . . Then you keep going, and it is fine.

You should have a sense of self-respect and self-comfort throughout your life. When you walk down the street, don't rush. Just take a nice walk. Be yourself, appreciate yourself. Even ap-preciate your subconscious thoughts. Appreciate that you are a human being in one piece. Your arms and your legs and your head are not flying off everywhere because of your wild thoughts, but you remain as one good human being with your shoes and your hairdo, perhaps wearing glasses, a tie and jacket, walking on the good earth, on the good street. Just do that, just walk nicely. Just do it. Then you will begin to feel that you are doing your *real* job. It's not even a job, but you are actually being what you should be. After that, you can learn to eat properly, drink properly, even pee properly. Everything comes from that basic sense of being and wholesomeness. You are one piece rather than disjointed. This is a very ordinary experience, which happens to people all the time, but they don't regard it as a good message. They just think, "Oh, forget it." According to the Buddhist teachings, people always have that flash of buddha-nature in them—always—but they don't acknowledge it. This is the same thing.

The wisdom of Shambhala is not the product of some accident. It's not that somebody just happened to do the right thing and now we are relaying their message to you. Rather, this wisdom has tremendous heritage and background. It comes from several thousand years of basic tradition, from a society of enlightened people, great warriors of the past. This tradition comes from Shambhala-oriented people who achieved this; in turn, they are so kind as to let us use their wisdom and to let us practice in this way.

We can find this wisdom even in the midst of the worst of the worst situations. The politics and policies in South Africa were terribly problematic for many years. However, South Africa still produced the Krugerrand, such a good gold coin. In any situation, there is always some dignity, some goldlike element. Tibet is a lost country, at this point. The Chinese occupied my country, and they are torturing my people. It is quite horrific, every bit as bad as South Africa. We Tibetans were unable to avoid that situation. Nonetheless, the Tibetan wisdom has escaped. It has been brought out of Tibet. It has something to say, something to offer. It gives us dignity as Tibetans.

On the other hand, however, although the West possesses tremendous technology, it comes along with enormous arrogance. Even though you are able to land on the moon, technology in itself is not a saving grace. We should appreciate the basic traditions of wisdom that have been preserved. It is absolutely wonderful to have respect for wisdom. You are not receiving the wisdom of Shambhala because you won the lottery. You come to this tradition with genuine interest and genuine respect. It's not random at all. It's not that you happened, by chance, to have the right number and therefore you are here. You aren't a subhuman being wandering around in a lost paradise, trying to find answers to your questions, hoping to bump into the right way to do things.

The training of Shambhala is geared to educate you to be an honest person, a genuine person, not fake. The sitting practice of meditation is the main vehicle to accomplish that, so I would like to reiterate the importance of practice. When you practice, hold your seat and have a sense of your breath, without questioning or slumping halfway through. Just let the breath flow. You are sitting on the earth. This earth deserves you; you deserve this earth. That is a very important point. The basic concept of joining heaven and earth is that you are there fully, personally, genuinely.

By practicing in that way, we come to experience the Shambhala teachings very directly. Our appreciation of the teachings brings a natural appreciation of the teacher. Because of our respect for wisdom, we can appreciate the spokesperson for the wisdom, the elder. *Elder* in this case does not mean someone who is chronologically old. Rather, it is someone who has worked and practiced and tested the Shambhala wisdom. It is someone who is able to survive in the world of the setting sun. In fact, such people are able to glow and project a good message that will influence others. It is quite remarkable that they are willing to share their compassion and their limitless kindness with others. There are such people, and that lineage and warrior tradition are worthy of respect. Often we think that we can buy wisdom. People have spent lots of money trying to do that, but they are unable to accomplish very much. It is very important to realize that wisdom cannot be bought or sold, but wisdom has to be practiced personally. Then we begin to realize the value of wisdom. It is priceless.

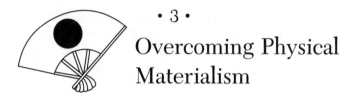

Overcoming Physical Materialism

In working with students in the Western world, I have been pre-senting a twofold message: first, how to overcome psychological and spiritual materialism; second, how to overcome physical mate-rialism. The first message is designed to help people become genu-ine practitioners in the Buddhist world. The second message is to help people overcome actual physical materialism by practicing the disciplines of body, speech, and mind so that they can become war-riors in the enlightened world of Shambhala.

IN CONNECTION WITH RENUNCIATION, we discussed the joy of basic goodness, the sadness of the setting sun, and the discipline of what to accept and what to reject. Out of that, we come to respect wisdom; therefore, love for the teacher or the elder may develop. Renunciation is also connected with overcom-ing habitual patterns such as early morning depression. With that understanding, I'd like to go a little bit further, although my ap-proach, generally speaking, is not to jump the gun. I don't want to present tricks or ways to overcome problems when you haven't undergone thorough personal training.

The next theme is letting go. From the discipline of renunciation, knowing what to accept and what to reject, and from realizing your basic goodness altogether, you begin to realize that you can let go. In order to introduce this theme, I'd like to tell you a story. In 1974, His Holiness the Sixteenth Gyalwa Karmapa, the head of the Karma Kagyü lineage of Buddhism to which I belong, was to arrive for his first visit to North America. A group of us had a meeting, and we talked about protocol and other arrangements. Quite a number of people said, "Couldn't we just take His Holiness to a disco and feed him a steak? Do we really have to vacuum the floor? Maybe he should sleep on a waterbed. Couldn't he just come along and see what America is like?" In the end, that wasn't the approach we decided to take! That would have been the opposite of letting go, which is not taking pride in one's crudeness. That approach is bloated with arrogance.

Letting go is free from the vision and style of the setting sun. Instead, it is connected with the idea that you are *worthy* to let go. If you are a good driver and you know the mechanics of your car, then you can drive at 110 miles an hour on the highway. You know how to control the car, how to work the mirrors and the steering; you know the power of the engine, the weight of the car, the condition of the tires and the road, the weather, and how much traffic there is on that highway. You may drive fast, but it does not become suicidal at all. It becomes a dance. Maybe it is quite dangerous for me to say that. I would not recommend that you play with letting go. But when you have the real sense of letting go, you should let go.

The Buddhist idea of wisdom is similar to letting go. *Samyak-sambuddha,*[1] the ultimate attainment of enlightenment, is corre-

1. A Sanskrit epithet for the Buddha that means "the completely perfect awakened one."

lated with somebody who can let go thoroughly. Such people have attained the wisdom and the skillful means to know how far they can push or develop themselves. Therefore, the daringness of letting go is connected with skill and training. If any of you are athletes, you know that. In a sport such as skiing, for example, if you start to let go at an early level of your training, you end up breaking your legs. If you mimic or ape letting go, you run into trouble. On the other hand, if you let go properly, once you have good training in how to let go and how to stop ambition and frivolity altogether, then you discover that you have a great sense of balance. Balance doesn't come from holding on to the situation. Balance comes from making friends with heaven and earth: earth as gravity or a reference point for us and heaven as breathing space where we can actually build up our posture and hold our head and shoulders properly. I've been riding my horse Drala every day, and I keep learning, again and again, that balance is not freezing your legs to hold on to the saddle. The balance comes instead from how much you float with the movement of the horse as you ride. So each step is your own dance, the rider's dance as well as the dance of the horse.

You have to be qualified to be daring, to begin with, but then, once you are qualified as a daring person, you really have to push. The obstacle might be thinking, "I may not be ready to be daring; I'm still not qualified." Such doubts happen all the time, but once you have made a basic connection to the notion of wisdom, you have to let go of those doubts. The Sanskrit term for wisdom is *jnana,* and the Tibetan term is *yeshe. Ye* means "primordial" or "intrinsic." *She* means "knowing." If you have that sense of primordially knowing what to do with your body, speech, and mind, then you should let go. Quite possibly you could supersede the levitation they practice in transcendental meditation, or TM. Of course, the Shambhala training is not about jumping up from our seats and glorifying *that*; we are concerned with floating properly.

39

When you trust yourself, gravity is no longer a problem. Gravity is already trusted, and because of that, you can uplift yourself. Yeshe: "wisdom" is the best English translation we've come up with. Yeshe is the achievement of wiseness or the craft and art of being wise.

Letting go is not that previously you were afraid and now you can relax or let go of your fear. It is something more than that. Letting go is being in tune with the atmosphere, the challenging world altogether. Our motto in Shambhala Training[2] is "Living in the Challenge." That is letting go: living in the challenge. This does not mean constantly being pushed and pulled, that your banker calls and says you have to put more money in the bank and your landlord says that you are about to be evicted. You could be living in the challenge that way, but we're talking about something better than that! The greater level of living in the challenge is that every moment is a challenge, but challenge is delightful. Letting go also means *daring* to go. It's as if your life feels like a firecracker, and you are waiting for the boom. That is daring.

First, you have a dot of goodness. You might hear a high-pitched sound in your ear, and that might be the sound of the dot, that very high pitch. *Any* first thought is the dot. Then, after that, you learn to proceed. The practice of life, a sense of joy, sadness—everything comes out of that first dot. Then, finally, you discover letting go. However, you don't just run wild. You learn the practical details of letting go: letting go in body, speech, and mind; letting go in your household and family conduct. Letting go is *manifesting*. It is giving up all your reservations. You may say, "Suppose I rent this apartment or this house. Will I be able to handle it?" Or, "If I move in with this man or woman, will the relationship be OK?" Any of those things is a challenge. Shambhala Training: living in the challenge!

2. The weekend meditation programs in which these talks were given.

I hope that people can appreciate their surroundings. Appreciate the autumn—which does not mean you have to go to New England to see the leaves. Appreciate winter, appreciate summer, appreciate spring. There are lots of things happening in your life. People's lives are full of things, including their loneliness. People are leading very full lives keeping up their apartment, cleaning the house, relating with their friends. There is always something happening. Anybody who possesses the five sense perceptions always has feedback. If you've overslept, you might be awakened by a blackbird chirping outside your bedroom window. The world is not all that empty. There has to be a drama; there has to be gossip; there has to be a visit from somebody or other. We are always creating tea parties or cocktail parties, inviting people over. That's a natural situation, which is very sacred and wonderful. Lately, we've been spoiled by television, whose creation is one of the worst crimes ever committed, I would have to say. When you watch TV all the time, you have your appreciation of self-exploration taken away. But apart from that, there are lots of situations of natural feedback. We hear sounds, if we are not deaf; we see visions, if we are not blind; we can talk, if we are not mute; and we can smell, and we can feel. All of those worlds around us are wonderful.

You can please yourself with the simplest detail, such as a fly landing on the tip of your chopsticks as you are about to eat. That is the best pun that one could ever think of. Life could be very simple and good in that way. When we appreciate such details, we are not becoming stupid or crazy or simpleminded, but we are becoming more visionary. One can imagine how Einstein would feel if he were eating with chopsticks and a fly landed on the tip of his chopsticks. He would probably have a laugh. So we don't have to solemnize our world, and we don't need a Merry-Go-Circus to cheer us up all the time.

41

BODY

The wisdom and daring of letting go come in three sections, which are very simple categories: body, speech, and mind. First is the body aspect of letting go. Usually, wisdom refers to being learned, roughly speaking. Here we are not talking about those logicians who have a logical answer to everything or about modern lawyers who can twist the truth to win their case. Rather, we are talking in terms of fundamental or *body* wisdom. Letting go is a sense of completely immaculate discipline, pure discipline. Why should we discipline ourselves? Not because we feel bad; therefore, we have to be disciplined like naughty children or, for that matter, like bad dogs who defecate on the rug and have to be whipped or have their noses put in the deposits. Discipline here is delightful.

This comes back to a topic that we've already discussed: working with early morning depression. That subject always comes back, I think. Sometimes you experience morning depression, and sometimes you might have early morning excitement, early morning vision. In either case, you don't exaggerate the delight or just flop down and reduce yourself into a piece of charcoal and breathe out black air. The key to avoiding either side of that mentality is to take care of your physical body, whatever happens in everyday life. When you wake up and get out of bed, the first thing you do, perhaps, is to go into the bathroom and look at yourself in the mirror. Your hair is disheveled, you look half asleep, and you see your baggy skin. You have a physical reaction. You say, with a big sigh, "Here we go again. I see myself once more today with a disheveled hairdo and bags under my eyes." You already feel pressed to get to your first appointment. But right at that point, while you're looking at yourself in the mirror, the discipline is to look yourself in the eye and pick up on the basic goodness possibilities. Then you can cheer up, as well as cheering up your inmate, your mate.

You see, creating enlightened society is not based on everybody riding on some big idea. Quite possibly, when terrorists have hostages, they wake up in the morning with a feeling of delight: "Oh, goody, we have *hostages* next door!" But in our case, we have basic goodness, not even next door but *in* us already. Our vision is not coming out of aggression, passion, ignorance, or any or those neuroses at all.

You may be living in a very difficult situation. Maybe your apartment is purely plastic, flimsy, and artificial, built by the setting-sun people. You don't have to live in a palace all the time. Wherever you are, it is a palace. About three months ago, I and some of my students conducted what is known as the Magyel Pomra Encampment[3] at Rocky Mountain Dharma Center.[4] We were living in tents, and there wasn't any running water. Of course not! We were camping out. At one point, there was a possibility that water would not be available to us at all. But we were able to enjoy ourselves anyway. We would wake up and wash in a basin; we did our exercises, hoisted our flags, blew our bugles, and we were *there*.

In North America, most places have quite a good plumbing system, which is a big advantage. Jumping into the shower or taking a good bath can be helpful in the morning. When I lived in England, the plumbing system was not all that efficient. Still, we made a good job of it. There's an English tradition that you can take an entire bath using one cup of water, particularly in the desert. You can be dignified, wear a nice uniform, and wash up with one cup of water, without wasting anything. There is a cer-

3. Trungpa Rinpoche established a yearly outdoor program in 1978 called the Magyel Pomra Encampment as a vehicle for teachings on mind training and overcoming aggression.

4. The Rocky Mountain Shambhala Center, a rural meditation center in the mountains above Fort Collins, Colorado, near the Red Feather Lakes, was previously named the Rocky Mountain Dharma Center.

tain wisdom in that. In that case, it's based on survival, obviously. At the same time, there is a sense of how to utilize your environment and do things properly.

We are not talking about buying Buckingham Palace so that we can relax. We can relax wherever we are. If you see an apartment where the previous tenants left a mess, if the rent is decent and you want to move in, you can spend at least fifteen minutes to clean it up. By spending lots of fifteen minutes, you can make quite a palace out of that situation. The idea of dignity is not based on moving into a red-carpeted situation. That will never happen. It *might* happen to people who can spend lots of money to make their homes into palatial situations, but even that is deceptive. If they have to do that, then they are creating an artificial court, an artificial palace. Things have to be worked on and done with our own bare hands. We have to do things on the spot, properly, beautifully, nicely. Even in the worst of the worst situations, still we can elegantize our lives. It's a question of discipline and vision.

The physical wisdom of taking care of yourself and your body is very, very important: what kind of food you eat, what kind of beverages you drink, how you exercise. You don't necessarily have to jog or do push-ups every day. But you should take the attitude that you do care about your body. The body is the extension of basic goodness, the closest implement, or tool, that you have. Even if you have physical defects of all kinds, I don't think there should be any problem. We don't have to feel imprisoned by disease or sickness. We can still extend ourselves beyond. In the name of heaven and earth, we can afford to make love to ourselves.

Sometimes people are very shy about that, particularly if they make too much reference to what is known as the doctrine of egolessness in Buddhism. People have heard about the renunciation of great yogis like Milarepa, and sometimes they think that, if they torture themselves, they will be following Milarepa's example. Somehow things don't work like that. The asceticism of practicing meditation in a cave is part of the yogic tradition. You can do that, but *before* you do that, you have to have enough strength and self-respect to starve to death in a cave in the name of the practice of meditation. One cannot use one's sloppiness as part of indulging in asceticism and self-denial. Living in the dirt does not work.

Many world religions have encouraged individuals to become monks or nuns. Although monasticism is very natural, in some sense, it's also a heightened or rarefied level of existence. In the Shambhala teachings, our main concern is working with society. We want to develop an enlightened society that will be based on the idea of pure letting go: the best society, where people will tell the truth, be genuine to themselves, have physical discipline, and take proper care of their children, husband, wife, brothers, sisters, and parents. There has never been proper instruction in how to become the best business owners, householders, parents, laundry-men—whatever you have. So we are talking about how to become a real person in the world and how to have a real enlightened society. There *is* such a thing as the Shambhala style of how to treat ourselves. That is learning how to be a warrior. I don't want to purely present philosophy, but I want to share my own training, what I do myself. I would like to tell you how you can actually become warriors, practically speaking, and how you can treat yourselves better so that we can have an enlightened society.

Self-respect is wonderful and glorious, absolutely excellent. Sometimes you get dressed up for special events. When you go to work the next day, you are bound to change into jeans, T-shirts, and overalls or whatever your work clothes may be. Please don't regard that as switching off your Shambhala dignity. You don't have to change your psychological approach due to a job situation or a shortage of money. You might think that you'll end up doing the "setting-sun trip," although you don't like it, because of economic problems. But you can still manifest fantastic dignity and goodness. You should have respect for your dirty jeans and five-times-worn T-shirts and your messy hairdo. Be in accordance with the notion of basic goodness and there's no problem. We could say quite safely that everything's in the mind.

The other day, several people came to me to receive a blessing. They came straight from work, so they had on their work clothes, and they were disheveled; but they had tremendous presence and grace. It was very beautiful. I was quite moved by it, actually. It is an interesting logic: physical appearance, treating your body well, and eating proper food are all very important, but at the same time, you don't have to overstate those things. You can be quite lovely and natural wearing jeans and T-shirts. On the other hand, there is the basic American Sportsman look. All these mail-order catalogues show you how to look nice while you're shoveling mud. Perhaps they've got something there, but obviously, the whole thing has become commercial. You can be a dignified person wearing a T-shirt and cutaway jeans, as long as there is a *spirit* of sportsmanship in the work that you're doing.

You might wake up in the morning feeling depressed, look around on the floor, and find the first clothes available to put on. That is a problem. You should have a wardrobe of some kind, based on what the occasion is. Animals don't have this problem. They are always prepared. When you are a dog, you're always a dog. When you are a horse, you're always a horse. Animals always look fine; sometimes we bathe them, but they don't have to choose their wardrobe. At the same time, their nakedness is different from human beings' nakedness. Human beings were corrupted a long time ago by putting on their pretense, costumes of all kinds. The American world is particularly conscious of that. You see signs in restaurants saying, COME AS YOU ARE. But then, they have to amend that with another sign that says, NO SHOES, NO SHIRT, NO SERVICE. That is a very interesting sociological dilemma. I think that's where the Shambhala teachings come in, with the understanding that dignity in one's physical appearance is very important.

SPEECH

The second category is speech and telling the truth. People often use speech as a method of asserting themselves in society. If you want to talk to somebody who doesn't speak English, for example, you often shout at him or her. Or if you want to express confidence during a job interview, you do your "speech trip"— which is not necessarily based on the truth. Sometimes you have to bend the truth to make yourself look better than you are, so that you will get a job. I sympathize with that, but the basic point of speech is communication.

In the vision of the Great Eastern Sun, your friends are regarded as brothers and sisters, so it is very important to feel connected and to communicate with them. You waste a lot of time by not saying what you feel. Then your friend is confused, and you are as well. To avoid that problem, your personal feelings should be expressed freely to your friends. Speech is also connected with gentleness. In the Shambhala world, you speak gently; you don't bark. That is as much a part of dignity as having good head and shoulders. It would be very strange if somebody had good head and shoulders and began to bark. It would look very incongruous.

MIND

I spent a longer time talking about the first wisdom of the physical situation. If you work with your body situation, speech and mind will come along with that. The final category of letting go is mind, which is connected with being without deception. Sometimes we waste a lot of time asking other people's opinion as to whether we should make certain decisions. "Should I ask somebody to marry me?" "Should I complain to that woman who was so rude to me?" "Should I ask my boss for a raise?" Of course, if you really need advice, it's fine to ask for it. But in many situations, we don't actually want someone's opinion; we're just expressing our lack of confidence. If you trust in your existence, you will be free from such indecision, which is a form of ignorance. Ignorance is indecisive; it is uncertainty as to how to conduct yourself. The only genuine reference point, as far as mind is concerned, is the pure understanding that basic goodness does exist. You can actually project out that sense of meditative state without second thought. Flash out that first thought free from fear and doubt.

Sometimes, when you are studying something, your mind goes blank. You can't even think. That is the fear of intelligence and the fear of not being able to connect properly. You're not a hopeless case, but you fear that you are. There is so much fear of wisdom that wisdom becomes monumental. To break that down, relate with your daily life situation, starting from the disciplines of body, speech, and mind. Then you will begin to realize that there is actually a spark of goodness in you that is known as the first dot. That dot is the source of fearlessness. When you have a dot, you may not necessarily be free from fear, particularly, but at least you are *awake*. Fundamental goodness is already there. Therefore, you begin to appreciate yourself. Then, because of that, you begin to feel that you're capable of working with others. So you develop individuality without individuality, which is an interesting twist.

From the appreciation for this wisdom, this particular dot of basic goodness, you begin to develop respect for hierarchy. The wisdom is genuine and it works, so one develops loyalty to the source of wisdom, the teacher. Realizing that you can actually permeate that wisdom to others, you begin to feel a longing to work

with your brothers, sisters, mother, father, in-laws of all kinds—
who need that basic goodness message. We can't be completely
selfish, just getting the Shambhala wisdom and keeping it for ourselves. That would be almost criminal. We have to work with others, absolutely. That will be your burden, if you like, and it's a
good burden. I've done so myself. I will continue to do so myself
until my death and even beyond my death. We have to help
others.

In Asia, the ideal of enlightened society came from a mythical
kingdom called Shambhala. We could also say that enlightened
society existed when the Buddha taught. When he proclaimed the
four noble truths,[5] enlightened society took place. There was also
an enlightened society in Tibet during the reign of King Songtsen
Gampo in the seventh century. Songtsen Gampo was regarded as
one of the best and most benevolent Tibetan monarchs, and the
enlightened world that he organized lasted about two hundred
years.[6] In India, the reign of Emperor Ashoka in the third century
BC was another example of enlightened society.[7] His goal was to
spread peace throughout the world, and he was the first person in
history to start hospitals, both for sick people and for animals.
Before that, there were no hospitals anywhere in the world. His
concept of a hospital was based on the bodhisattva ideal of sympathy for others and working for others' welfare. In the medieval
world, religion and politics were not all that separate. Also society
was not all that organized in those days, but still these enlightened
societies did take place.

5. The four noble truths were the first teaching given by the Buddha after his
enlightenment. They are the truth of suffering, the truth of the origin of suffering,
the truth of the cessation of suffering, and the truth of the path. A brief summary of
these teachings is that all life is filled with suffering; that grasping or desire is the
source of suffering; that enlightenment, or the cessation of suffering, is possible; and
that there is a path or a way to free oneself from the endless cycle of suffering.

6. For further information, see the entry for Songtsen Gampo in the glossary.

7. Additional information on Ashoka can be found in the glossary.

The idea of decency in the medieval world was very fuzzy, but in the modern world, the border is very distinct between enlightened society and unenlightened society. So in modern society, the creation of an enlightened society, such as that of Emperor Ashoka or King Songtsen Gampo, is highly possible. In the medieval world, hardly anybody could write or read. These days, most people are literate, so they have access to all kinds of written messages, making it possible to share things with people on a much broader level. In medieval times, people suffered less from physical materialism, but the line between comfort and discomfort was marginal. There was not very much comfort and not very much discomfort. People were hardened and vague from that experience of the world. Today, in most parts of the world, comfort and discomfort are much more distinct and sharp. At least suffering is much more pronounced, although pleasure may still be vague. There is much more room to teach people the truth of suffering. If you understand that truth, there is more room to bring about enlightened society. So the current century brings vivid possibilities.

The basic point of this training is to work with the rest of the world, to liberate their aggression, and to provide a gentle world that will work. A lot depends on your individual participation, so that you can graduate from the setting-sun world to the world of the Great Eastern Sun and become a full-fledged Great Eastern Sun person. The definition of the Great Eastern Sun is threefold:

- *Radiating confidence, peaceful:* The Great Eastern Sun radiates the peaceful confidence of nonaggression. Second is:
- *Illuminating the way of discipline:* We've talked about that already: learning what to accept, what to reject, and how to develop discipline and wisdom altogether. Then, the third part of the definition is:
- *Eternal ruler of the three worlds:* That is connected with the idea that you cannot get away from the light. If you are part

of the greenery—a flower, say—and you want to grow, then you always need the sun as your king. Ruling your world here is also connected with developing the wisdom of body, speech, and mind. Those are the three worlds. Ruling is also the idea of joining heaven and earth together, so that the world is one world.

When the truth is taught, a lot of people find it threatening. In many cases, truth is told with apology. But in presenting the Shambhala teachings, we are telling the truth without apology— truth without apology, with dignity and honesty, top to bottom. I am so proud and happy that people can respond to *real* truth, without philosophy, without a pep talk. It's unheard-of! I'm so honored. I suppose we might be thankful to the setting-sun world. Because it has been so powerful in our lives, by contrast, we have come to the discovery of these Great Eastern Sun possibilities.

Personally, I am trying to live up to what I've been brought up as: a Tibetan gentleman who has no particular concern other than helping others. When I came to this country in 1970, I met very intelligent people. At the same time, they were so gullible. They were willing to buy any spiritual trip. So my first message to them was, "Please, be critical. Don't buy anything that somebody says. Question them. Try to develop critical intelligence." That is the notion of cutting through spiritual materialism. I wrote a book by that name,[8] which was geared to help people realize that you don't just follow any spiritual teaching. That had become a problem, and it had created tremendous pollution in the American spiritual world.

Beyond that, of course, we have physical materialism, which was not particularly mentioned in that book. But it *is* mentioned here. We have to overcome physical materialism, which is think-

8. *Cutting Through Spiritual Materialism* was published by Shambhala Publications in 1973.

ing that wealth or possessions will relieve our suffering and make us happy. Fundamentally, that is what we have been discussing here: how to retrain ourselves and how to restrain ourselves, very simply, from physical materialism.

So in working with students in the Western world, I have been presenting a twofold message: first, how to overcome psychological and spiritual materialism; second, how to overcome physical materialism. The first message is designed to help people become genuine practitioners in the Buddhist world. The second message is to help people overcome actual physical materialism by practicing the disciplines of body, speech, and mind, so that they can become warriors in the enlightened world of Shambhala. I hope that you will regard the Shambhala world as a big family. You are all invited to join this particular family. In the Buddhist world, we talk about joining the family of the enlightened ones. Here we are talking about joining enlightened society. Everybody is quite welcome.

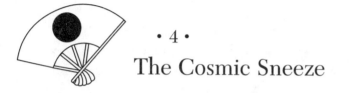

· 4 ·

The Cosmic Sneeze

Wherever there is a junction in our experience, the primordial dot occurs. Before experience becomes hot or cold, good or bad, there is a junction where the primordial dot occurs. The primordial dot has no bias to either that or this; therefore, it is unconditional. It is the mark of existence of human being and of the challenge of the human heart. Before the challenge, there is it. It's like hearing a big bang, like the explosion of a cannon. You hear a bang, and then you wonder whether that bang is going to kill you or celebrate with you. One never knows. Usually, it's neither. It's just a big bang.

AS HUMAN BEINGS, we have a tremendous bond, a tremendous connection together. Having made the basic discovery that we are decent human beings, we are ready for a further discovery. Whether we are delivered or yet to be delivered from the sickness and degraded situations of the setting sun, we are ready to discover the Great Eastern Sun vision.

The Shambhala training is a study of cultural situations—not in the sense of studying another language or another lifestyle, but in the sense of learning how to behave as human beings. We are endowed with head and shoulders; we are endowed with our sense perceptions and our intelligence. We can work on ourselves, and we can communicate with others. We are adorned with a brain and heart, so that we can be intelligent and also soft and gentle. We are capable of being harsh. We are capable of being soft. We are capable of being happy, and we are capable of being sad.

We often take these human attributes for granted, or we may even think they get in our way. People often talk about trying to hold back their tears, but as human beings, we should take pride in our capacity to be sad and happy. We mustn't ignore the preciousness of our human birth or take it for granted. It is extremely precious and very powerful. We cannot ignore our basic human endowment. Nonetheless, it is not a gift, nor is it purely the product of our own hard work, either. It is simply basic existence, which is contained within us. It is known as the primordial dot.

The primordial dot is the basic purity and goodness that everybody possesses. It is unconditional; that is why it is called *primordial.* It is free from the stains of habitual patterns, and it is free from our educational training. It is free from our childhood upbringing, and it is free from the trials and errors of our everyday life struggles. The primordial dot is the origin of everything, and that is why it has no origin. We can quite safely say that we cannot tell which came first, the chicken or the egg. Or in this case, we could say that neither did. The dot is not even one. It's zero.

We have to learn to think differently. You see, things are not always made. Ultimately speaking, there's no artificer. I think that's a theistic bias that some of you may have, if I may say so. But there *are* situations that are not made by anybody at all. When we try to describe this dot, we have to say something about it, and that makes it sound as if it does exist. But even the word *existence* is inadequate. That is why we call the dot "unconditional." It is beyond our conception. It is before we ever conceived of *I* and *am* at all. This primordial dot is fundamentally *it,* and it is pure, and therefore, it is *good. Good* in this case refers to unconditional goodness, free from good and bad, better and worse. There is a unique and unusual, fresh, and basic situation that we have, which is the essence of warriorship, the essence of human being. It is unconditional primordial goodness.

We call it a *dot* because it occurs very abruptly in the situation, on the spot. It cannot be traced by scientific examination or by an alpha machine. It is just a dot, which always occurs. The dot occurs when we are uncertain. If you are driving quite fast and you see an intersection up ahead and you are uncertain which way to turn, at that point, there is a gap and the dot occurs. Then there is an afterthought: "Turn right," or "Turn left," or "I'll have to take a guess." The dot occurs when you feel sad and you wonder, "Will I burst into tears, or can I hold back my tears?" The dot occurs when you see a person. "Should I frown or smile?" There is indecision, and the dot occurs. That is the human condition. It does not tell you exactly what to do.

At the junction of that and this, the human condition is expressed as a challenge. Therefore, it has been said that this primordial dot is the source of fearlessness and also the source of fear or terror. Sometimes you find the dot is petrifying, without any reason. Sometimes you find it makes you quite heroic. One never knows where the fear or the courage comes from. It's almost at the level of an infant's experience rather than anything metaphysical or conditional. It's as simple as jumping into the shower and finding that the water is cold or hot. The water temperature is not your state of mind. A cold shower is a cold shower. A hot shower is a hot shower. Where did it come from? It's very direct. Unconditional goodness, the primordial dot, is free from any neurosis. It's 200 percent truth. That's it! It's hot or cold, which is not particularly a product of neurosis at all.

If you try to figure out what I'm talking about logically, it will be almost impossible. Look at the fickleness of mind, waving like a flag in a strong wind. You have a sudden stop, and the primordial dot occurs, in the form of either confirmation, indecision, or whatever it may be. It is like a military march, where the drill sergeant shouts, "COMPANY . . . !" The primordial dot occurs. Then, the sergeant may say, "Left wheel!" which is after the fact. It could be any command: "COMPANY . . . Attention!" "COMPANY . . . Halt!"

When the gong rings as you begin the sitting practice of meditation, when the gong rings as you finish your sitting practice, the primordial dot occurs. When you're about to drink a cup of coffee in the morning, wondering whether it's sweet enough or has enough cream in it, whether it's hot or cold, as you bring the cup of coffee toward your mouth, as your lips quiver and protrude to touch the cup of coffee—at that very moment, the primordial dot occurs. It is the essence of humanity and warriorship.

Wherever there is a junction in our experience, the primordial dot occurs. Before experience becomes hot or cold, good or bad, there is a junction where the primordial dot occurs. The primordial dot has no bias to either that or this; therefore, it is unconditional. It is the mark of existence of human being and of the challenge of the human heart. Before the challenge, there is *it*. It's like hearing a big bang, like the explosion of a cannon. You hear a bang, and then you wonder whether that bang is going to kill you or celebrate with you. One never knows. Usually, it's neither. It's just a big bang.

The dot is the beginning. Can you think of any other ways to describe it? Splash? Square? Dash? Any one of them might do, after the fact. It is a dot, just *touch*. It is like saying "NOW," particularly in the English language. *Now. Here.* You could say "dot," or you could say "BANG," if you like. Visually, it's a dot; audibly, it might be a bang. It's quick, precise, and pinpointed. If we trace back in the Buddhist tradition, there is a term, *bija,* which means "dot word." *Om, ah,* and *hum,* for example, are what are called *bija mantras.* Such a dot, or bija, is onomatopoeic, just one shout, a cosmic sneeze. Trusting that such a primordial dot does exist in us is not a matter of belief. It's not something you've been taught and therefore you believe it. In this case, you experience it as so. Therefore, it is trustworthy. It is always one dot. Always. You can't have several dots; otherwise, it becomes a relative dot.

Having had the primordial dot experience, you can join that with the practice of warriorship, the Shambhala journey. When you put the dot and the practice together, then you will know the best way to conduct yourself. The primordial dot is the essence or strength, but by itself, it is not particularly a help or a harm. It's just potential. You have your guts; you have your heart; you have your brain. But then you say, "What can I do with such a fantastic brain, an excellent heart, and excellent guts?" You can't do very much if you don't have any path or journey to follow. That's where helping others and developing yourself comes into the picture. When you have a yearning, a sympathetic attitude toward yourself and others, and a willingness to become genuine, then the primordial dot becomes a somewhat conditional primordial dot. Then you have a path; you have a journey.

The path and practice of the Shambhala training are how to cultivate the primordial dot as a creative situation. We shouldn't exactly say "cultivate" the dot. We can say that we *have* the dot; therefore, we take advantage of it. We can't really cultivate it. It was cultivated a long time ago. We have it, and then the question is what we will do after that. When we open our eyes, the first thing we see is the horizon. We see light. Similarly, having experienced the dot, we feel a breeze of fresh air, and we can proceed. Through the warrior's subsequent training process, the first dot becomes helpful, a way to wake yourself and others up.

Trusting in the dot means actually having to make friends with an unconditional situation. It arouses your intention to save yourself as well as others from misery, confusion, and darkness. It is like the Buddhist notion of the bodhisattva: that you are going to be benevolent and help others. You are not going to fall asleep, but you're going to use your direct understanding of the primordial dot to help others. To do so, you have to believe in freedom, liberation. Nobody is completely blind to the primordial dot, at all. Everybody has at least a quick, short, tiny glimpse of that primordial dot. So no one is hopeless. It is our duty to realize that. The dot is potential, the potential to do *anything*. Freedom is the path, working with the dot and applying that potential. *Free* is the pure experience of the dot, and *dom* is the action that arises from that. *Free* is first flash, first thought, and then *dom* is second thought. The warrior principles of genuineness, decency, and goodness, with excellent head and shoulders, all lead us to work with others. Here, basic goodness is no longer a theory or a moralistic concept. It is direct and personal experience. Therefore, we can trust in liberating the setting-sun world altogether.

The primordial dot is free from bias of any kind; it is guileless. Therefore, we can make a connection with people, including ourselves. As we progress further and further, we realize that what we are being taught is so real, much closer to actual reality. Maybe at the beginning there was some element of make-believe or conmanship, using our aspiration to arouse our potential warriorship. But as we progress, we witness actual magic, manifest on the spot: we are worthy of being human beings. Then we can no longer lie back and say, "What a relief! Now that I've heard about the primordial dot, I can relax." Instead, we develop further ambition to open ourselves to work with others. We declare ourselves as the diaper service, garbage collectors, janitors, taxi drivers—the laborers to serve humanity.

You probably know, more than I do, that this world needs

tremendous help. Everybody's in trouble. Sometimes they pretend not to be, but still, there's a lot of pain and hardship. Everybody, every minute, is tortured, suffering a lot. We shouldn't just ignore them and save ourselves alone. That would be a tremendous crime. In fact, we *can't* just save ourselves, because our neighbors are moaning and groaning all over the place. So even if we could just save ourselves, we wouldn't have a peaceful sleep. The rest of the world is going to wake us up with their pain.

I don't see any particular problems in working with others. Just go ahead. Push yourself harder. Sometimes you find that you don't like someone you are trying to work with. But if you look behind their facade, you see that the person is, in fact, quite lovable. They do possess the primordial dot. When you first talk to them, you might find them completely off-putting and irritating. You wouldn't touch them with a ten-foot pole. But gradually, your pole becomes shorter. You begin to do a double take; you might even begin to like them. The point here is that you have to push harder, and then there's no problem at all.

You might be working with somebody who is completely untrustworthy, but that doesn't matter. Trust begins with trusting in yourself, your dot, and your commitment. You have to work hard to help others, directly, without even wearing rubber gloves to clean up their vomit. You're not like an employer who is interviewing potential employees to decide which ones to hire. We are going to help others, regardless of their workability. That is not particularly our reference point. The point is to just be precise and ordinary with everyone, yourself and others. When we talk about working with others, we are talking about working with *ourselves* to begin with. If we are ready to work with others, it doesn't matter *who* comes along in our world. One has to do it, one can do it, and one should do it, because we have that particular tendency known as basic goodness. We have that first thought to flash onto the situation. We are highly well equipped to help others.

Having trust in freedom, or liberation, comes from having conviction in our primordial dot. The experience of the primordial dot also brings inscrutability so that we don't become so upset by the pain of the world that we're paralyzed by it. We don't break down completely, but we maintain our head and shoulders so that we are capable of helping others. The practical means of realizing all of this is the sitting practice of meditation. Without experiencing the practice, you may have difficulty understanding what I'm saying. The practice of meditation can help you to understand the purpose and reasons for your being in the world. Practice will help to answer some of those questions, although it will also leave a lot of questions unanswered. That ground where answers and uncertainty come together will be our working basis.

Discipline in the Four Seasons

There is a time for restriction. There is a time for opening. There is a time for celebrating. There is a time to be practical and productive. Basic natural hierarchy operates that way, and the vision of the Shambhala Kingdom is based on those principles.

THE SHAMBHALA IDEA OF RENUNCIATION is being free from laziness as a whole. When the students of Shambhala feel that they have to be mindful twenty-four hours a day, sometimes they wish that they could take short little breaks, here and there, and just indulge and let go in the negative sense. Sometimes they think, "In the good old days, I used to be able to do everything. I could even take pride in degrading myself." That temptation to lower oneself down into subhuman level is what is renounced.

We have already discussed the importance of working for others. Working for others inspires us to work further on ourselves by renouncing the neurosis of the setting sun. Then, the neurosis that others indulge in is no longer our reference point or our temptation. Because we already have an understanding of our basic goodness, we have acquired some protection from being brought down into the lower realms. And having experienced the primordial dot, we know that we are well equipped to work with ourselves and others. Nonetheless, being mindful and alert all the time is quite difficult, so there might be temptations. Therefore, renunciation is a key point. However, renunciation is not going back to a gray area, but it is a celebration. It is experiencing the joy of basic goodness. That is what brings renunciation.

There is tremendous self-destructive and perpetual pain that comes from missing the point in the setting-sun world. The logic of the setting sun is based on cultivating pleasure, seemingly. But the end product is that, by seeming to cultivate pleasure, you inherit pain. The setting-sun outlook is based on indulging in your sense perceptions. It is being carefree and careless, which may be caused by being very wealthy, very poor, or by just being mindless. Out of desperation, you run to the nearest entertainment arcade, but you leave with a long face. Nothing has really entertained you, and you leave feeling disappointed. The Buddhist tradition talks a great deal about the nature of *samsara*, or conditioned existence, and how indulging one's ego and trying to glorify oneself produces more pain rather than pleasure of any kind. So studying the setting-sun approach is absolutely necessary as part of the development of renunciation. Understanding the setting sun brings further inspiration for working with others, and it also connects you further with the primordial dot.

Through the sitting practice of meditation, a person becomes well trained in day-to-day mindfulness and awareness. You become very sharp and precise, naturally alert, and very inquisitive and powerful. You develop a clear understanding of the neurosis of the setting sun. Its falsity is seen through, but you do not develop resentment of setting-sun people. There is no one-upmanship. Rather, you develop an understanding of the setting-sun world and a willingness to work with it. In working with others and with yourself, you must be willing to get your fingers dirty. You are willing to taste the situation fully. It's like being a doctor. As a doctor, you don't have to get your patients' diseases in order to help them. But at the same time, a doctor is willing to look at you from the inside out, to go inside you to find your sickness and try to cure you.

There could be dangers, of course. You don't adopt the setting-sun vision or become involved in its indulgence. But on the other hand, you don't become arrogant. You can't say, "We are the Great Eastern Sun people, and we will never touch you." Seeing how arrogance might develop while you're working with others brings a sense of humility. Humility, very simply, is the absence of arrogance. When there is no arrogance, you relate with your world as an eye-level situation, without one-upmanship. Because of that, there can be a genuine interchange. Nobody is using their message to put anybody else down, and nobody has to come down or up to the other person's level. Everything is eye-level.

Humility in the Shambhala tradition also involves some kind of playfulness, which is a sense of humor. At the beginning, communicating with somebody may be somewhat flat, but the sense of humor in the relationship is always lurking around the corner. Instead of approaching things flatly, you may have to scan around to the right and the left, to see whether there are any sparky areas where you can communicate. So humility here is slightly different than in the Catholic tradition. In most religious traditions, you feel humble because of a fear of punishment, pain, and sin. In the Shambhala world, you feel full of it. You feel healthy and good. In fact, you feel proud. Therefore, you feel humility. That's one of the Shambhala contradictions or, we could say, dichotomies.

Real humility is genuineness. It's not even honesty. Honesty implies a twist of punishment or negativity—that you have drawn the card for deception, put it in your pocket, and now you'll draw another card for honesty. But there's only one genuineness, which is being oneself to the fullest level. The willingness to work with others is what is known as *discriminating awareness,* or *prajna* in the Buddhist tradition. It is the basic idea of sharpness. *Discriminating* in this case does not mean accepting the good and rejecting the bad. It is seeing light and dark, the disciplined and the undisciplined states of existence, very clearly. Because of that, one knows what to accept and what to reject in one's personal existence. For instance, one would not indulge in the setting-sun style. One would avoid that. One would take up the Great Eastern style of warriorship. But the discipline of acceptance and rejection is not the product of love and hate.

Renunciation provides a tremendous open space for us. It shows us how to handle ourselves and how to relate with dichotomy and paradox. On the one hand, there is one taste: we have to jump into the world and work with people, sacrificing ourselves as much as we can. On the other hand, we have to stay pure. There is no fundamental contradiction at all, as long as our approach, or first thought, is in contact with the primordial dot. Through the manifestation of the dot in the way of the warrior, we gain the natural discipline of how to stay awake, clear, and elegant. We receive tremendous courage, which we call fearlessness. Then we are able to work with others and handle the world of the setting sun.

There is no such thing as a failed warrior. Either you're a warrior, or you're a coward. When the warrior fails, he becomes more and more petrified by his surroundings, and he ceases to be a warrior. He is even afraid of his own sword. On the other hand, not succeeding is the warrior's staircase to discovering further bravery. Cowardice provides all sorts of challenges. When you become a warrior, fearlessness is your first discovery. Then, the next discovery is the gigantic roadblock of cowardice. You feel petrified, and you want to run away. At that point, the warrior should realize the nature of fearlessness in himself or herself and step on that problem. Rather than frightening you away, cowardice becomes a staircase. That is how a warrior is made out of a coward.

Realizing that the Shambhala wisdom is not purely the product of human concept gives rise to further humility. The Shambhala world is discovered by tuning in to the law of nature. We may complain about the hotness of the summer and the coldness of winter. Nonetheless, in the back of our minds, we accept that there has to be summer, winter, autumn, and spring. In the same way, there is natural hierarchy. Leadership is part of the principle of hierarchy. We are grateful that wisdom is available to us. We feel so fortunate to be students of the Shambhala discipline, to have a student-teacher relationship, and to discover human hierarchy as well. We can participate in the Shambhala world; we can discipline ourselves; we can receive teachings that are being offered by a particular teacher. Such a situation of natural hierarchy almost feels as if it were organized by the four seasons.

After we have had an entire winter, then comes spring. Things begin to thaw, and we can appreciate the little warm breezes of the season. Then, as the plants and flowers begin to blossom, we begin to appreciate the warm summer, with its rain and thundershowers. Then, if we indulge too much, there is autumn, which restricts our summer indulgence. We have to harvest the grain to survive for the rest of the year. Then, having worked hard to harvest our crops in autumn, the last heat of summer turns again into the cold of winter. Sometimes it may be too cold. Still, it is helpful to see icicles and snowflakes and deep snow. They make us think twice about our life. Nonetheless, we are not eternally imprisoned by winter. Spring comes again, and then summer, autumn, and winter return all over again.

The four seasons have a natural hierarchy of restriction, openness, celebration, practicality—and then restriction again. We could talk about the functioning of governments or any organization, in fact, in the same way. Organizations have to have the restriction of a winterlike situation. In our Shambhala organization, for example, when we sit on our zafus, our meditation cushions, it might be painful for our legs and back. There is some kind of harsh winter taking place there on the cushion, but we come along anyway. Then, after we sit, we might gather together for a group discussion, and we begin to thaw out. We have spring there, thawing out the stiffness in our back and the pain in our legs. Then we have a summer celebration: sharing our wisdom, working together on projects. After the celebration of summer, we review what we have done and how we have conducted ourselves, which is the fruition level of autumn. We become very busy with our evaluations, and we feel so good, until finally, we are back to our zafu of winter.[1]

There is a time for restriction. There is a time for opening. There is a time for celebrating. There is a time to be practical and productive. Basic natural hierarchy operates that way, and the vision of the Shambhala Kingdom is based on those principles. In contrast, a democratic society would vote out winter if it could. Some political systems might want to have nothing but winter or, for that matter, spring, summer, or autumn. Obviously, they are not literally changing the seasons, which is the saving grace. But whole societies have been organized with no thought given to natural order or law, and the result is complete chaos. The early forms of communism tried to maintain the winter of restriction the whole year round, put together with the productivity of autumn. When those societies began to produce more material

1. The author is describing how a typical program at a Shambhala practice center might include these different aspects of the four seasons. He could be describing Shambhala Training or other programs sponsored by the Shambhala organization. However, these principles can be applied to the functioning of any organization or government, as he goes on to point out.

goods, then the communists wanted to have summer year-round. Capitalistic countries such as the American world want to have the celebration of summer all the time, with a touch of autumn's productivity. Other liberal political systems, which are partially left or right, may want to have the thawing-out process of spring all the time. In that situation, the society takes care of everything, so there is a hint of a coming summer celebration, but basically the reference point is derived from getting away from the harshness of winter. At certain times, any of those systems work, just as each of the four seasons works at a certain time of year. But none of those systems works for a whole decade, not even for a whole year.

The hierarchy of natural order is that human beings should enjoy what they have and be given what they deserve. At the same time, you are encouraged to grow up. You cannot be an infant or a teenager for the rest of your life. So natural hierarchy is also connected with renunciation, in that one has to *yield* to some system of discipline. We also have to work with the four seasons, quite literally. Some people think it is a great idea, if they like summer weather, to fly around to wherever the summer is. When it gets too cold in the north, they go south for the winter. When it gets too hot in the south, they return north. That is a dilettante and nouveau riche approach. According to the Shambhala principles, we have to be deeply rooted in the land: we stay where we are and work with what we have.

In connection with discriminating awareness wisdom, in the Shambhala tradition, we value our trade or profession. It expresses our unique capability. It is our source of economy, or livelihood, and our means of working with those around us. So we don't change professions constantly, but we stick with what we do best. If you are an author, you remain an author. If you are a jeweler, you remain a jeweler. If you are an actor, you remain an actor. We take pride in our individual resources, which come from the primordial dot. We have been given certain abilities and ways to express ourselves. We were born or woke up with certain particular abilities, and we stick with them.

In some sense, this calls for tremendous renunciation. It is so tempting to change your occupation now and then. Five years of this, six years of that, ten years of this, three years of that, this and that, that and this. If you pursue that mentality to the nth degree, you can end up living out of a suitcase, going everywhere, back and forth, not accomplishing anything, meeting lots of people and writing back to them later, after they've even forgotten your name. You become a wanderer in the wrong sense, not like a monastic wanderer or a mendicant. Rather, you have lost your ground, and you have no real trade of any kind.

The setting-sun world encourages that. You bump into a business opportunity, and with a certain amount of good luck, you can make millions of dollars in a few years. You get thoroughly spoiled by that. Then you experience tremendous depression when the economy changes, and the market for your product is gone, switched into something else. Or somebody else comes up with a better idea than yours, and your millions of dollars are gone. You're penniless, and your morale is gone. Your warriorship is gone. Now you're back to square one, trying to come up with another good idea. You're so spoiled. If you keep going that way, you become nothing but a hungry ghost in the degraded world.

Of course, you may be able to keep on successfully reproducing your world, becoming richer and richer. But at the same time, you are losing your dignity. You have no self-respect; you don't value sacredness; and you sink further into the ground, hour by hour, month by month. You age very quickly from the strain and the depression of being too rich. We should realize and recognize those setting-sun tendencies. If we respect natural hierarchy, we will find that there is order and a kind of self-government that allows us to neither indulge nor not indulge, but to open ourselves and jump into situations and discipline ourselves thoroughly.

STUDENT: I was wondering if the government of Shambhala would have a constitution?

DORJE DRADUL OF MUKPO: Certainly, there is a constitution. If you study the four seasons, they have a very complicated constitution. If you study the human mind, it has a constitution. Buddhist psychology, or the *abhidharma*,[2] provides a very complicated description of how the human mind works and what remedies can be applied at particular levels of the human mind. But in the Shambhala world, the constitution doesn't seem to be the main point. The main point is the natural organicness of the situation.

STUDENT: So, then, the situation determines the form rather than trying to lay a form onto a society?

DORJE DRADUL OF MUKPO: That's right. Yes, very much so. For example, we needed to have the lights switched on here tonight. If we didn't switch them on, it would be too dark to have a talk. But we don't all go over to the light switch together. We designate somebody to switch the lights on. We all agree that it's nighttime, it's too dark to have a talk in this hall, and we need light. Then somebody is appointed to go over to the switch and turn on the lights. That is constitution for you.

---

2. The abhidharma—literally, the "special teaching"—represents the earliest compilation of Buddhist philosophy and psychology. It is a codification and an interpretation of the concepts that appear in the discourses of the Buddha and his major disciples.

· 6 ·
Mirrorlike Wisdom

Coming to the Western world, I encountered the makers of the clocks, big and small, and the makers of other machines that do wondrous things—such as airplanes and motor cars. It turned out that there was not so much wisdom in the West, but there was lots of knowledge.

OUR BASIC THEME is still the primordial dot. From that dot, the open sky dawns, which is to say, great vision arises and expands. Trust arises out of that, and from that trust arises the need for renunciation. Because of renunciation, we can be *daring,* which is the principle of letting go.

In the ordinary sense, *letting go* means being carefree and giving up any discipline. It means to hang loose or to stop being square. It can have the connotation of going against the societal norms you were brought up with, whether it be the Protestant ethic or Orthodox Jewish ethics. In modern-day Catholicism, some of the monastic traditions are becoming more informal. For instance, a priest may not use the confessional box to hear confession. Instead of wearing a habit, monks and nuns might dress in lay clothes, maybe even jeans. Instead of saying mass on the sanctified altar, priests might conduct the ceremony in the middle of the church. Instead of speaking or praying in Latin, they now use the colloquialism of their national tongue. Instead of having organ music, the church might invite jazz musicians to present their own songs as prayers.

The Shambhala approach to letting go is more like having an excellent running conversation in Latin or Sanskrit. Or it is how to speak the English language properly, with tremendous feeling. Letting go is the eloquent expression of speech, the expression of dignified existence. With body loose and available, it is highly controlled awareness joined with inquisitive and open mind. Those are the expressions of letting go.

This is not *my* version of letting go at all. I do not take personal credit for it, nor should I. It is purely my upbringing as a Shambhala person. As a child in the monastery in Tibet, I was brought up very strictly. At the age of five, I began to study and learn to read, write, and think. While I was learning the alphabet, I was taught to sit up properly. I was told that it is bad for you to hunch or lean over when you are memorizing the alphabet. I was told that my handwriting would be like my posture, so I shouldn't hunch over. I was warned that my pronunciation would also be bad if I didn't sit up straight. I was told, "Sit upright, read with upright posture, and write with upright posture."

I was never allowed even the shortest break of any kind. All preoccupations or excuses were completely undercut. I had a private tutor, so I was the only person in the schoolroom. There were no other students to compare notes with or to have as a reference point at all. In this country, I suppose, if you were put in such a situation, you would think it was a torture chamber. But starting from the age of five, I went along with my life and my surroundings. I was not intimidated by the sternness of my tutor, and somewhere in the back of my mind, I realized that there was something right about this stern education and training of a young boy of five years old.

My tutor was like my parent. He attended me constantly: he helped me dress, and he served me food. He even escorted me to the toilet, which was somewhat claustrophobic—because you're hoping to take *some* time off. Twenty-four hours a day of discipline. My tutor slept in the same room with me. If I had a bad cough and I woke up in the middle of the night, he would also be alert. He was always ready to serve tea, water, or anything I needed. So he was a good servant, as well as a very unreasonable teacher. He was usually very stern, with occasional affectionate remarks.

Such an education is very rare these days. The closest thing in the Western world, I suppose, would be the British public school system, but even there, nowadays, they have relaxed the system enormously. In any case, that approach is somewhat insensitive and Victorian in style. In this country, such a system of educating a child is nonexistent.

The parents of the fifties and sixties felt that their strict table manners and discipline had failed. Many of their children rejected them and became revolutionaries or hippies or did all sorts of strange things. The parents took this on themselves and thought they had done a bad job of raising their children. Moreover, they felt out of date and too old-fashioned to fit into the modern world. Some of the children reformed, if I may use that word lightly, and they reconnected with their parents, so the older generation felt somewhat better because the children became more reasonable or conventional than they used to be. But the parents still felt they had done a bad job. So some of them, in turn, loosened up in the wrong sense. They gave up the dignity of their earlier days, and they, too, learned to dress sloppily. They rejected their silver chandeliers and sold their crystal glasses at garage sales, and they purchased a plastic kitchen set, unbreakable.

While I was growing up in Tibet, I was so attracted to the American way of life and the Western style of doing things. I thought that Westerners must have a very subtle wisdom and etiquette. They knew how to build airplanes, complex machines, and fantastic wonders of scientific technology. With such wisdom in the gadgetry world, I thought that the makers of the gadgets must have a similar personal discipline.

I was given my first watch when I was fourteen years old. It was from England, and I couldn't resist opening it up to see how it worked. I took it completely apart. I tried to put it back together, but it no longer worked. Then I was given a clock that chimed. It was a gift from another Tibetan teacher, another rinpoche, who incidentally was the brother of one of my main teachers in Tibet: His Holiness Dilgo Khyentse Rinpoche. Everything worked perfectly inside this clock, so I decided to take *it* apart. I wanted to compare the parts of the clock with all the mechanical parts that I had previously disconnected in my wristwatch. I laid the parts from both timepieces side by side and tried to figure out how these machines worked, how they actually hung together.

When I took the clock apart, I could see the mistakes I had made with the watch, and I was able to put the clock back together. In fact, I got both of them back together, I cleaned them, and they worked better than before. I was quite proud of that. I thought that the Western world must have *such* discipline, minute precision, profound detail, and patience, based on all those little screws that had to be screwed in. I thought somebody had made each little piece with his or her own hands. Naturally, I had no concept of factories at that point. I was very impressed, and I had a great deal of respect.

Then, coming to the Western world, I encountered the makers of the clocks, big and small, and the makers of other machines that do wondrous things—such as airplanes and motor cars. It turned out that there was not so much wisdom in the West, but there was lots of knowledge. Moreover, everything seemed to be based on the notion of a warning system. People were afraid of getting hurt, afraid to even go outside without wearing a coat and hat, in case they might catch a chill. Englishmen in particular always go out with their umbrellas, whether there is rain or not.

My first exposure to the Western world was in Britain, where I went to university at Oxford. I'm afraid my respect for Western daringness thinned out a little bit, but I retained tremendous respect for the accuracy I encountered. I met many scholars in Oxford and elsewhere in Britain. I found that they wanted to be very accurate in their understanding of Sanskrit or Buddhism or their own traditions. I took a course in comparative religion and also a course in contemplative practice in Christianity while I was at Oxford. I found the presentations to be somewhat technically oriented rather than wisdom-oriented. The only wisdom-oriented Christians I met were some Jesuits, who were very interesting. One of their main purposes is to convert non-Christians to Christianity. The particular Jesuits I met were interested in converting *me* to Catholicism. Many of them had been to Sri Lanka, India, or other parts of Asia.

The first Jesuit emissary to Tibet was sent by the pope in the eighteenth century. This Jesuit priest was told first to study the language and then to have a debate and win the Tibetans over. He actually wrote a book about his experiences. After the debate, nobody was converted. The reason nothing happened was because of his exposition of the resurrection of Christ from the dead. In the Tibetan tradition, there is a term for somebody who rises from the dead. It refers to a ghoul. Unfortunately, that's the term the priest used. So when he was explaining how Christ rose from the grave, the Tibetans thought he was talking about worshiping a ghost, which horrified people.

Coming back to the point, our Shambhala training has actually come from the older generation's wisdom, from an even older generation than the parents of the fifties. Our current upbringing and educational systems might be obstacles to daringness. Obviously, it is impossible for you to uneducate or deeducate yourself completely. You don't have to, but your system of thinking has to be changed into the Shambhalian point of view. That is to say, you should not be afraid of ignorance or stupidity.

When we discussed renunciation, we talked about not being afraid of setting-sun people. This is similar. The first point of daringness is to take pride in yourself. Even if you forget what you've learned, due to not being mindful, you don't panic. You will recover what you've forgotten if there is a sense of self-respect. Suppose you forget the name of your best friend who saved your life forty years ago. You are telling your life story to someone, and suddenly you go blank. You don't remember the name of the person who saved your entire life. You don't panic because of your knee-jerk stupidity and ignorance. That person's name is bound to come back to you, sooner or later, unless you don't let go. If you keep trying to think of that person's name, you might forget it eternally.

So we shouldn't be afraid of our own forgetfulness. When you are frightened by something, you have to relate with fear, explore why you are frightened, and develop some sense of conviction. You can actually look at fear. Then fear ceases to be the dominant situation that is going to defeat you. Fear can be conquered. You can be free from fear if you realize that fear is not the ogre. You can step on fear, and therefore, you can attain what is known as fearlessness. But that requires that, when you see fear, you smile.

The Tibetan word for a warrior is *pawo*, which means "a brave person." If you don't work with a situation properly, you might hurt someone, which is the mark of cowardice and impatience. People kill an enemy on the spot because they feel they can't be bothered, which is a mark of laziness; because they hate someone so much they want to see them die, which is a mark of ignorance; or because they would like to strike the person dead, which is a mark of aggression. The warrior, pawo, would never do that. Challenges are the working basis. That is why we have a world. If you slaughter everybody in the whole world, you have nothing left to work with—including your lover. There's nobody left to play with or dance with.

I don't want to sound arrogant, but I do feel that the training I've gone through is very worthwhile. I'm so grateful to all of my teachers and my tutors. I'm utterly grateful to them—at least at *this* point! By creating the Shambhala training, I'm trying to provide each of you with a similar training, as much as possible. Obviously, you don't each have an assigned tutor to follow after you. It would be somewhat difficult to provide that. Instead, you are expected to be your own tutor and to be extremely watchful—not by looking out for danger but by being open and disciplined.

The final topic is wisdom, which is connected with an appreciation of hierarchy. Once you have discovered hierarchy or a sense of universal order, you have to tune yourself in to that. You have to make yourself available and attune yourself to that situation. That is very important. Tuning yourself in to the hierarchy of the Shambhala world means that you are willing to fight or create obstacles or at least to reform the setting-sun political systems, using whatever capabilities you have. We are not talking about having marches or anything like that. But in your own life situation, you have to realize and resist the setting-sun demands to have winter throughout the year, summer throughout the year, autumn throughout the year, or spring throughout the year. You have to recognize the problem of being one-dimensional or cultivating only one season in your life, and then you have to allow some system of wisdom to enter into your state of existence.

We are talking about how to work with very simple situations, such as talking to your landlord or landlady about the rent, consulting with your bank manager about taking out another loan, depositing money in your checking account, buying another house, doing your grocery shopping at the supermarket, or dealing with your dry cleaner. Whatever situations you are working with, you have to be aware that every step you take is very precious. You cannot change this world into the Great Eastern Sun world with a snap of your fingers. It can only change stitch by stitch. What thread you use, what kind of needles you use, and how you sew the fabrics together—that is purely up to you.

You might feel that this is such a small-minded approach that it will have almost no effect at all. Particularly if you are gung ho on Shambhala vision, you might be so impatient, thinking that this is taking too much time and won't have any effect. But that is not the case. We must go step-by-step, starting from square one. Pay attention to your environment, to your relations with your landlady, your landlord, your grocery store, your bus, every place you go, everything you do habitually. Look at them twice, thrice. How you deal with the cockroaches in your apartment, how you vacuum your floor, even how you flush the toilet: any dealings that you have with the outside world, so to speak, have to be witnessed thoroughly and watched very carefully. You do not need a tutor like I had. You have hundreds of tutors around you. All those situations are your tutors, and they will give you the message.

Wisdom is not purely the product of intelligence. You have to work on things personally. It's not exactly hard work, but it's taxing in some sense, because you have to be constantly alert, all the time. The notion of wisdom is the same as prajna, or the discriminating awareness that we discussed earlier in the context of renunciation. I am using the word *wisdom* here because what you are being given is something that can only be taught to you in the form of a hint. Having been given the hint, you pick up the message spontaneously. That is wisdom.

Wisdom is what joins heaven and earth. You bring your zafu and *zabuton,* your meditation cushion and your meditation mat, together for the sitting practice of meditation. When the gong rings, you and your cushion are joined together. That is joining heaven and earth. I'm putting it on a very elementary level. Joining heaven and earth is not like making a decision. It is the principle of a mirror. You have electricity or daylight, which is heaven. You have your body, your face, your uncombed hair, your beard—which are all earth. Then you have the mirror, which joins together that heaven and earth. When you look in the mirror in the daylight, you can comb your hair nicely; you can shave your beard properly. So wisdom is the principle of a mirror.

I had an interesting conversation with someone about the movie *Star Wars.* There is a famous phrase in the movie, which is "May the force be with you." It's rather like saying, "May energy be with you." That is not a scientific approach. You just take a certain attitude, and by assuming that attitude, you accomplish the whole thing. When I heard that phrase in the movie, I was very excited, because it reminded me of the presentation of the Shambhala principles. Dot: force. You don't have to be scientific about it. At this point, if you need a reminder, the dot will be your password. When you have a dot, you are not even in the junction, but you are on top of the situation. Think of a dot in space. Dot.

Whoever makes the final and primordial connection with the dot will be the king or queen of Shambhala who joins heaven and earth. But there is not even a king. There is just the dot. The dot king. Just a tiny black dot who is the king of Shambhala. It is possible that people can achieve that, in the same way that we talk about enlightenment. How many buddhas will there be? How many kings and queens of Shambhala will there be? It is saying the same thing.

I don't think any of those kings and queens will go dotting off on their own, because their dot is actually a calligraphy. You need paper and ink to make a dot. The ink and the paper are the subjects of Shambhala, who are the ground of physical discipline, psychological discipline, and speech discipline, accomplished all together. Because the ground of discipline exists, therefore, the king or ruler can exist. Dot exists, but it is not a human creation.

Try to practice and think about what has been discussed here. I have tried to be as straightforward, honest, and genuine as one human being can be in talking to another human being. I think you know that. My heart has softened toward all of you so much. I love all of you. Thank you.

GOOD MORNING WITHIN THE GOOD MORNING

Because of my forefathers,
Because of my discipline,
Because my court, the tutors and the disciplinarians, have been
    so tough with me—
You taught me the Shambhala vision.
I feel enormous gratitude.
Instead of sucking my thumb,
You taught me to raise head and shoulders.
With sudden unexpected eruption,
I have been blown into the cold land of a foreign country.
With your vision, I still perpetuate the discipline you taught me.

On this second occasion of the Shambhala Training of Five,
I would like to raise a further toast to the students and their
    practice:
May we not suck our habitual thumbs,
May we raise the greatest banner of the Great Eastern Sun.
Whether tradition or tales of the tiger,
We will never give up our basic genuine concern for the world.
Let there be light of the Great Eastern Sun
To wake up the setting-sun indulgence.
Let there be Great Eastern Sun in order to realize
Eternally there is always good morning.

*Written on the same day that the talk "Mirrorlike Wisdom" was
given.*

PART TWO

BRILLIANT

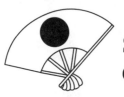

· 7 ·

Sacredness · Natural Law and Order

When you experience that there is such a thing as basic goodness and that things are in a natural order, you realize that there is no natural evil. There's no fundamental evil trying to destroy the world. On the contrary, you begin to feel that you are being protected and nourished, even cherished, by the norms of natural order. Then you can respond to situations quite naturally. You respond to the four seasons. You respond to color. You can always relate with the natural goodness that does exist.

IT IS MY INTENTION, basically speaking, to make the Shambhala training available to the world independent of any demand for a spiritual or religious commitment. The commitment that is needed is individuals' desire to elegantize their lives. In order to survive and maintain our elegance and, positively speaking, to maintain our arrogance, one of our main concerns should be how to lead our lives fully and properly, as we deserve to. We can choose to lead our lives on the basis of confidence, fearlessness, and elegance. Tomorrow is Halloween. If we can be genuine tonight, we could surpass the possibilities of dressing up as somebody else for Halloween.

I would like to revisit the principle of basic goodness. Basic goodness: Why is it basic? Why is it good? We are not talking here about choosing good over bad or having allegiance to a good idea as opposed to a bad idea. We are talking about *very basic* goodness, which is unconditional. *Unconditional* means that goodness is fundamental. You don't reject your atmosphere; you don't reject the sun and moon and the clouds in the sky. You accept them. The sky is blue. You have your landscape; you have your cities; you have your livelihood altogether. Clouds are not regarded as for or against you. Sunshine is not regarded as for or against you. Fundamentally, there is nothing threatening you, and nothing is promoting you either. That is fundamental goodness, natural law and order.

The four seasons occur free from anybody's demand or vote. Nobody can change that universal system. There is day; there is night. There is darkness at nighttime. There is daylight during the day, and nobody has to turn the light switch on and off. The survival of human beings is based on this natural law and order, which is basically good—good in the sense that it's sound, it's efficient, and it works, always. If we didn't have the four seasons, we wouldn't have crops, we wouldn't have vegetation, and we couldn't relax in the sunshine. We couldn't enjoy home cooking either, because there wouldn't be any food. We often take this basic law and order in the universe for granted, maybe too much so. We should think twice; we should appreciate what we have. Without it, we would be in a completely problematic situation. We couldn't survive.

Basic goodness is *good* in the sense that it's so basic and *therefore* it is good, not in the sense of good as opposed to bad. It is good because it works. It is a natural situation. The same thing could be said of our own state of being, as well. We have passion, aggression, and delusion. We cultivate our friends, we ward off our enemies, and we are occasionally indifferent. That setup is not regarded as a shortcoming of human beings, but it is part of the elegance and the natural equipment of human beings. We have every faculty we need, so that we don't have to fight with our world. And because the world is not particularly a source of aggression or complaint, therefore, it is good, and we are good. We can't complain that we have our eyes, ears, nose, and mouth. We can't redesign our physiological systems. For that matter, we can't redesign our state of mind, which comes along with the physiological systems anyway.

We have been equipped with nails and teeth to defend ourselves against attack. We've been equipped with our mouth and genitals to relate with others. Fortunately, we are also equipped with our intestines and our colons, so that food can recirculate: what we take in can be flushed out. Those natural situations are wonderful—ideal, in fact. Some might say it is the work of a divine principle. Maybe. But those who couldn't care less about divine principles still have to work with this natural situation.

We should feel that it is wonderful to be in this world. How wonderful it is to see red and yellow, blue and green, purple and black. All of these colors are provided to us. We feel hot and cold. We deserve these things; we *have* them. Basic goodness is what we have, what we are provided with, the natural situation that *everybody* has earned from their childhood up to now. Fundamentally speaking, it is not good in the ordinary sense of good, good, goody, good. Neither is it particularly bad. It is unconditional.

The setting-sun world tries to manipulate basic goodness and make it into basic badness, saying that everything in the world is evil, including the four seasons, and everybody is trying to destroy each other. The setting-sun tradition even tries to revoke the creation of the world. According to the Christian tradition, God created everything at its best, as much as he could, for human beings. The setting-sun world is a democratic world that is always complaining and trying to redo God's design of the world and the rest of the universe (except on weekends and the Sabbath, when it can be very convenient for setting-sun people to take a rest). But when you experience that there is such a thing as basic goodness and that things are in a natural order, you realize that there is no natural evil. There's no fundamental evil trying to destroy the world. On the contrary, you begin to feel that you are being protected and nourished, even cherished, by the norms of natural order. Then you can respond to situations quite naturally. You respond to the four seasons. You respond to color. You can always relate with the natural goodness that does exist.

Basic goodness is basically *it*; therefore, it is good—rather than it is good as opposed to bad. So the first part of relating to basic goodness is appreciating that we have it and learning to apply our intelligence to manage or maintain that goodness. In a sense, we are learning how to take possession of basic goodness. It is not our possession, but nonetheless we have it, and we deserve it. And therefore, we can trust in basic goodness, which is the next topic.

Trust is the absence of neurosis, and trust is the epitome of well-being. Trust is also the essence of ideal comfort. Once again, we are talking about something very basic—in this case, *basic* trust. When you trust in goodness, you are making a connection with reality: with the rocks and the trees, the greenery, the sky and the earth, the rivers and the fires, with everything that exists around you. You can always trust that blue will be blue, red will be red, hot will be hot, and cold will be cold. Trust also exists on a larger scale: you trust in the law and order of human society, which is that way because of *natural* law and order.

As your trust in natural order and law evolves, you find that you don't need extra entertainment to make yourself comfortable.

You don't have to seek simple, trivial, and ordinary ways to keep yourself occupied. You can simply relax. So in that way, trust brings relaxation. When we take reality for granted, we are always seeking new entertainments, new ideas, and new ways to kill boredom. You get bored with an old trust, so you have to find a new trust. That is the essence of the setting-sun approach. You've had enough of whatever you possess, so you look for something new. You abandon old friends, give away your old equipment, throw away old clothes, and come up with new clothes, new gadgets, new friends. There is no loyalty and no exertion involved with that approach. You might even get tired of the rocks and the trees, the rivers and the mountains, the sun and the moon. You might have to move to another planet. Even then, you might get tired of your new planet. What are you going to do then?

Someone may eventually figure out how to completely change the four seasons. Maybe they'll do that at Disneyland some day. You would pay to see *that,* no doubt. They might build a big dome over that fantasy world. In the middle of summer, they would create an ideal winter for you. In the middle of winter, they would create ideal summer for you. Human beings can be very tricky.

The opposite of that approach is to develop patience. In the English language, *patience* ordinarily means "to wait and see," "to endure the wait." In the Shambhala context, patience means *to be there.* It is simply being there, always being there. There is no connotation of being *so painfully there.* Patience is simple continuity and predictability. When you trust the natural sense of predictability, then you are patient, willing to be there. It's very straightforward and natural. Just be there. Just be there.

Out of patience comes joy. Realizing that you don't need any fresh, new, extraordinary things to entertain you, you can be there on the spot and celebrate what you have. You don't need new objects of appreciation. To witness and experience what you have is good enough. In fact, it's wonderful. It's already a handful, so you don't need anything extra. Actually, in that sense, it feels more like a sense of relief than joy. You also feel healthy. When you are not searching for a substitute or a better alternative to what you have, you feel quite satisfied. That brings natural health and wholesomeness. Unhealthiness comes from searching for alternatives. The satisfaction of basic health is appreciating ourselves and what we have already, naturally speaking. We accept the world of heaven, earth, and human beings.

The Shambhala wisdom respects the sacredness and the beauty of the world. We don't try to change the color of the sky. There are all sorts of little tricks to make our world different. Instead of blue, you might like a red sky, or you might like to paint your beige bedroom bright red. But you don't have to do that, and you don't have to change yourself for the sake of boredom. You never get tired of having two eyes. If you get bored with having one nose and two eyes, you might want to exchange an eye for a nose. Or you might want to have lips on your eyes. You don't have to do that. You can actually accept what you have, which is wonderful already. Therefore, joyful satisfaction comes with patience.

When you feel satisfied, you become free from laziness, which brings exertion. Being free from laziness is not cranking something up. It is simply being meticulous, absolutely meticulous. You don't leave dirty dishes in the sink. That's the level of freedom from laziness we are talking about. You clean up after yourself. You appreciate all the details that are involved in cooking a meal, relating with your friends—your mate, your parents, your brothers and sisters—or relating with the bank, the garbage collector, your shoes that need to be shined, your clothes that need to be pressed.

In many cases, domestic life is purely regarded as a hassle. People feel that their time is too precious to spend on domestic details. If having an important job makes you feel that you work at a higher level of evolvement and that housework is beneath you, that is a setting-sun approach. Although you can afford to pay a housekeeper and order her or him around, telling the person to clean things up for you, the Shambhala training is interested in helping you to clean up your own life. That doesn't happen by paying somebody to mow your lawn, clean your clothes, and paint your house. You have to do some of those things yourself. Freedom from laziness does not come from spending a lot of money to send everything to the laundry because you can't be bothered to wash your own clothes. You send your clothes out to be washed, hoping that they'll look good when they come back—but usually they don't. You can't use money to become free from laziness. You have to actually clean up after yourself and pay attention to every detail. You have to look into things personally. That approach will save you a lot of money—which is beside the point. It saves you from a lot of setting-sun possibilities, and out of that meticulousness comes genuine exertion. Understanding that nobody is going to add up your sums for you; you do the adding up yourself.

Then, although we may be free from laziness and gain exertion, beyond that, there is still a sense of cowardice or general anxiety. We feel a general nervousness about leading life, dealing with our livelihood, and working with others—our friends, lovers, parents, or anyone else. The only thing that corrects that situation of nervousness is to feel that both you and your environment are fully included in sacredness. You're not just an ordinary Joe Schmidt or Suzie Jones trying to lead a reasonable life. According to the Shambhala vision, you are sacred, and your environment is also very sacred. The sacredness is not from the point of view of religiosity. Rather, because you pay so much attention to your environment and because you are so concerned about the details as well as the general pattern of your life, therefore, the environment and the discipline that you have are extremely sacred.

When you develop faith or conviction in that sacredness, then, no matter what you are doing, you will find that different kinds of messages are evolving. When you pay attention to details or to your lifestyle in general—whenever you pay attention to the basic realities—nature begins to speak to you. It dictates to you, so you have a natural reference point happening all the time. In every ordinary life situation as well as in extraordinary life situations, there is always feedback from the environment as well as from your existence. This brings real fearlessness.

Fearlessness is the absence of cowardice. That is to say, cowardice, or uncertainty, comes from speed, from not being on the spot, and from not being able to lead life properly and fully. You miss a lot of details, and you also miss the overview. To correct that, you need *room* for fearlessness, which comes from having faith in your existence. Basically speaking, fearlessness is not particularly a reward or a goal, but fearlessness is part of the journey on the path. Fearlessness alternates with fear, and both of those are kindling for the fire. You are nervous, speedy, fearful. Then that brings another area of steadiness, solidity, and calm. So fear and fearlessness constantly alternate.

The end product is natural victory. Nervousness is not particularly bad. It is just a growing pain, a teething pain. Out of that, ultimately speaking, we find that we are steady, perceptive, and aware of details. At the same time, we begin to discover total basic goodness. Finally, that allows us to understand the true meaning of freedom. Often discipline makes people feel claustrophobic. They feel that the discipline is so big and personally invasive. They feel they have to get into this *thing*, called "The Discipline." That feeling can kill the spontaneity and the freedom that exist. Freedom doesn't mean that people should be free to do anything they want. But when we apply discipline, we should feel that it's spacious rather than that it's being dictated to us from just one angle. Then we will feel that we actually possess the world of heaven, the world of earth, and the world of human beings. It feels so spacious. Therefore, we delight in our practice rather than feeling that we've been sucked into a little vacuum.

When you were told to do certain things in school or when your parents told you to do something or perhaps when you were involved in other spiritual traditions, people made you feel guilty and bad. You were told that the only way to learn was through constant correction. There is so much punishment involved in learning. You're bad; therefore, you'd better be good. If you are a bad speller, you're told how bad your spelling is, so that you will learn to spell properly. If you can't maintain your composure during a dance performance, you're told how clumsy you are. Therefore, you'd better work hard to be a good dancer. That kind of logic is frequently used to educate people, and it has affected a lot of you.

Shambhala education is education without punishment, absolutely. Many people have tried that approach but find it quite difficult. They often end up punishing people anyway. It's tricky, but I think it's quite possible. We can be free from the mentality of praise and blame. We can create the world of basic goodness, that world that is good altogether, and nothing in that world is detrimental or problematic. To start with, there is an area of *good white.* Then, in the middle of that, you put a little dot, which is the good yellow of the Great Eastern Sun.[1] That should make you smile.

1. The author is describing the Great Eastern Sun pin that students in Level Five of Shambhala Training receive.

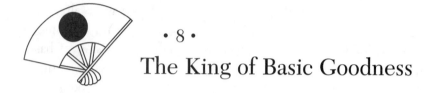

· 8 ·

The King of Basic Goodness

Because we know what to accept and what to reject, therefore, we are ready to fully join the world of basic goodness. That particular world is ruled and managed by a king or queen, who is capable of joining heaven and earth together. When we talk about a monarch here, we are talking about that which rules the world in the form of basic goodness. From this point of view, we regard basic goodness as the king or queen.

WHEN YOU ARE THOROUGHLY SOAKED in unconditional goodness and open mind, you become extremely insightful, knowing what to reject, and what to accept, and also understanding the basic notion of discipline. That brings renunciation.

The Shambhala idea of renunciation is very personal. It has nothing to do with giving up something bad, harmful, or trivial. Renunciation is necessary to make oneself more available, more gentle, and more open to others. The barriers between oneself and oneself and between oneself and others are removed. The basic temptation to take time off is also removed. Any hesitation and any form of warding off or putting up obstacles in order to maintain one's privacy are removed. We renounce our privacy, for the sake of both others and ourselves. Therefore, renunciation has a sense of sacrificing one's own privacy and personal comfort, as well as the temptation to take time off, take a break.

Having realized the universal possibilities of unconditional goodness and seen that there is already natural law and order, we begin to feel somewhat claustrophobic, because we realize that basic goodness is impossible to possess personally. You can't make a pet project out of basic goodness. The greater vision of basic goodness may seem like a fantastic idea. Nonetheless, sometimes you feel that you need to localize it somewhere. Basic goodness is such a good thing to have; therefore, you would like to own it and put your initials on it. You think that you would like to take just a little pinch and keep it in your pocket, a little piece of basic goodness to nurse in your own little pocket. So the idea of privacy begins to creep in. At that point, it is necessary to renounce the temptation to possess basic goodness. You can't hold it in your pocket or put your seal and your initials on the dotted line of basic goodness.

Renunciation means giving up a localized approach, a provincial or personalized approach. Sometimes, when we experience vastness, we feel that it is too vast. We need a little shelter. We need a roof over our head and three little square meals to eat. That's one of the ways the setting-sun concept came about. Although we realize the Great Eastern Sun is vast and good, we can't handle it. So we build a little kiosk, a little home, to capture it. It's too bright to look at directly, but we'd like to take photographs of it, put them in a square picture frame, and keep them as a memory. I suppose the idea of tourism came from that, too. So the idea of renunciation is to ward off small-mindedness of that type.

Renunciation relates to both what to ward off and what to

cultivate. It takes place in the atmosphere of basic goodness, with patience, without laziness, and with faith, as we discussed in the last chapter. Moreover, the environment of renunciation comes from the environment of the sitting practice of meditation. In meditation practice, you watch your breath, and you regard thoughts as purely your thinking process, your thought process, without punishing them or praising them. So while thoughts that may occur during sitting practice are regarded as quite natural, at the same time, they don't come with credentials. The Sanskrit word for meditation is *dhyana;* the Tibetan term is *samten*—which both refer to the same thing: steady mind. Mind is steady in the sense that you don't go up when a thought goes up, and you don't go down when it goes down, but you just watch things going either up or down. Whether good or bad, exciting, miserable, or blissful thoughts arise—whatever occurs in your state of mind, you don't support it by having an extra commentator.

Sitting practice is very simple and direct, and in the Shambhalian style, it is very businesslike. You just sit and watch your thoughts go up and down. There is a background technique, a physical technique, which is working with the breath as it goes out and in. That automatically provides an occupation during sitting practice. It is partly designed to occupy you so that you don't evaluate thoughts. You just let them happen. In that environment, you can develop renunciation: an ability to renounce extreme reactions against your thoughts or for them. When warriors are on the battlefield, they don't react to success or failure. Success or failure on the battlefield is just regarded as another breath coming in and going out, another discursive thought coming in and going out. So the warrior is very steady. Because of that, the warrior is victorious—because victory is not particularly the aim or the goal. But the warrior can just be—as he or she is.

There are three categories or principles of renunciation that I'd like to introduce. I try to be kind and not present too many categories, but these will actually enable you to think constructively.

CARING FOR OTHERS

Caring for others is the first level of renunciation. What you reject, or renounce, is caring completely for yourself, which is regarded as selfish, or for that matter, shellfish: carrying your own hut, your own shell, your own suit of armor with you. According to the traditional Buddhist stories of karmic cause and effect, lone ladies and lone lords may reincarnate as tortoises or turtles, who carry their own homes around with them. So *selfish* and *shellfish* are synonymous. That's what we have to avoid.

Caring for others means that you have to be stable within yourself. The ground for that is being *free from doubt.* Having experienced the trustworthiness of basic goodness, therefore, we have faith in goodness, which brings the freedom from doubt that is necessary in order to care for others. When people think about helping others, they often worry that, if they open themselves up, they will catch other peoples' germs and their diseases. They wonder, "What if we open up too much? What is the self-defense mechanism?" So the first thought people have is, What are they opening themselves up to, and how can they protect themselves? But if you are without doubt, that in itself is protection. Then you can open yourself fully to others, with gentleness, kindness, and caring—which brings daring. Caring for others, free from doubt, brings daring. Got it?

Daring is the result or the active aspect of fearlessness. When you experience a lack of fear, then what you *do* with fearlessness is daring, or letting go. Because you care for others, you have fearlessness, you have faith, there's no doubt, and you become daring. Traditionally speaking, even the most savage animals have developed gentleness and loving-kindness toward their own young. With that logic, any one of us is capable of being kind to others. Let alone when our motivation comes from basic goodness! That brings many more possibilities of being kind to others and being daring.

To work for others, a certain amount of gallantry is necessary. In other words, you have to rid yourself of crude anxiety, which you do by trusting yourself more. You learn to trust yourself by having a good experience of being by yourself. During this portion of your life, you might spend a lot of time alone, being by yourself and practicing sitting meditation, which *is* being by yourself. At this point, you don't need others to help you; you just need to be by yourself.

When you are able to overcome crude dissatisfaction and anxiety, then you don't need to look for any further extraordinary revelations. You can actually launch yourself in working with others right away. Working with other people has two facets: it's not just helping somebody else, but it has an effect on you as well. By working with others, you learn how to pull yourself together at the same time. To do so, you have to be genuine. You have to have been working on yourself for some time, so that others will have trust in working with you. When they express their frustrations to you, you don't completely freak out or try to avoid them. You have to be patient and understanding, which only comes from being somewhat soaked in working with yourself. I think that applies in any kind of educational system anywhere.

KNOWING WHAT TO ACCEPT AND REJECT

Daring to work with others brings insightfulness, or intelligence, which leads to the second principle of renunciation: knowing what to accept and what to reject for the benefit of others. Caring for others doesn't mean that your open, kind heart is willing to let any diseases in existence come into you. You have to be very healthy at the same time. To maintain that type of healthiness, we have to know what to do and what not to do. But we can't be hard-nosed about it; we don't become aggressive or paranoid people or, for that matter, hypochondriacs. We can't do everything that's available, nor should we do nothing. We have to choose. Acceptance and rejection, in this case, are not an expression of your partiality toward one thing or another; they are much more unconditional than that, and they are a mark of intelligence. Our intelligence provides a way of sorting out what to do, what not to do. Out of that comes *gentleness*. We know what to accept for the benefit of others and what to reject for the benefit of others. Therefore, our entire life, our entire existence, including our out- and in-breath, is dedicated to others.

THE KING OF BASIC GOODNESS

The third principle of renunciation is quite interesting. Because we know what to accept and what to reject, therefore, we are ready to fully join the world of basic goodness. That particular world is ruled and managed by a king or queen, who is capable of joining heaven and earth together. When we talk about a monarch here, we are talking about that which rules the world in the form of basic goodness. From this point of view, we regard basic goodness as the king or queen. It is almost an entity in itself, not just a metaphysical concept or an abstract theory of natural order.

Another way of putting this is that what joins heaven and earth together is the king or queen, and therefore, it is basic goodness. In other words, if there is natural law and order, the principle of royalty, or the principle of the monarch, already exists. Because the principle of the universal monarch joins heaven, earth, and human beings together, therefore, we can join our body and mind together as well. We can synchronize mind and body together in order to manifest as Shambhala warriors.

97

The conventional idea of a monarch is based purely on the heaven principle. In the West, when the industrial revolution happened, it was regarded as the utterance of the earth. In that situation, earth is completely opposed to heaven, so there shouldn't be any monarch. The logic goes that, if you want people to be happy and have good salaries, if the workers are to be treated well, there shouldn't be any heaven. There should be purely earth. In the Shambhala tradition, however, as well as the traditions of imperial China, Japan, and India, it is necessary to have a king or queen in order to join heaven and earth together. The Chinese character for the king is three horizontal strokes with one vertical slash in the middle, which represents heaven, earth, and human beings joined together. When people have lofty ideas that they aspire to, they do not fall into the depressions of practicality alone. At the same time, to avoid purely having lofty idealism, you need the working basis of earth.

Communism has suffered a lot from not being able to join heaven and earth. The communists started out being earthy people. "Workers of the world unite!" However, when the communist empire developed—as in Russia, for instance—the communists could not help creating heaven: a *vision* of communism. Subsequently, the only way they have found to bring heaven and earth together into a balanced situation is to copy capitalism. It's not quite heaven, exactly, but to them, it might be the closest thing. Capitalists believe in religion, and capitalists have more decorations on their military uniforms, more flags. In the beginning, the communists regarded those things as absurd. Later, they began to have all kinds of ribbons, bars, and uniforms. Look at what Mother Russia has produced. So coming to the point: they don't really know what they're doing!

On this planet earth, there has been a problem of joining heaven and earth, which produces tremendous chaos. Moreover, there is a problem joining mind and body together. Synchronizing

mind and body together is a *very* big deal in the Shambhala tradition. I recommend *kyudo,* the Japanese art of archery; the tea ceremony; and flower arranging as Eastern disciplines to help synchronize mind and body together properly. From the Western tradition, I would recommend the discipline of horseback riding in the dressage style as a practice to synchronize body and mind. Dressage is a unique discipline, very sane and enlightened, that trains you in how to synchronize mind and body together. I'm sure there are a number of other Western disciplines that can help to join mind and body together.

In summary, the three principles of renunciation are: (1) Having a kind attitude toward others, free from doubt, brings daringness. (2) Realizing what to accept and what to reject brings gentleness. (3) Realizing that the monarch joins heaven and earth; therefore, our body and mind are synchronized together.

In the study of Shambhala principles, the king principle, the principle of royalty or monarchy, is shown at its best, before it's been corrupted. Royalty in the Shambhala world is not based on creating a Shambhala elite or a class system. In that case, I wouldn't share the Shambhala vision with everybody. I wouldn't be telling you about this at all. I would probably have selected ten or twenty people to hear about the universal monarch who joins heaven and earth rather than discussing this openly. Why should I tell you these things? One of our topics, gentleness and opening up, has something to do with it. Every one of you can join heaven and earth. You could be a king or queen—every one of you. That's the switcheroo, the great switcheroo. That's why the entire vision is shared with everyone. That is a very important point. I feel neither apologetic nor arrogant about sharing the ideal concept of the kingdom with you. It seems quite natural: everybody should know how the trees and plants grow and how they experience hierarchy in the four seasons. You can all see how the ultimate ruler conquers the universe—which is something more than a medieval king or a temporal king.

We don't have many kings and queens left on earth these days, and many of those we do have seem to be on their way to becoming private citizens, anyway. Nonetheless, in any business and any organization, including educational or social ones, human beings have found that they still need a manager or a director of some kind. Hierarchy develops out of that. If you want to set up a restaurant, you need a manager, who is the king or queen. Then you can have waitresses and waiters and other employees as the ministers of the realm. Then you have the king's workers, which is the public. If you own a business, your investors might be regarded as the ministers, and you are the king or queen. At a bank, the king or queen principle is the bank manager, and then you have all the various other parts of the court represented by various positions. Organizational systems always work that way, but we are shy of pointing it out. The approach of Shambhala vision is to acknowledge hierarchy but to insist that people throughout the hierarchy—high, medium, or low—learn to conduct themselves in the Shambhala style. The highest in rank do not exert their power from arrogance but from a sense of humbleness, genuineness, and sympathy. It goes right on down the line that way.

Hierarchy is already there. Whether you are in a completely democratic or a communist system, you still cannot help having a manager in your restaurant. Wherever you go in the world, they always have those systems, which human beings have found to be the best working basis. You always have a Chairman Mao or a Castro in the communist world, and you have a president of the United States, in spite of democracy. A democracy still has a president. If a country were truly democratic, there wouldn't be any leaders at all—which can't happen. A country can't run that way. An organization can't run that way. There is always hierarchy.

But hierarchy has been mismanaged and misused. The ambi-

tion of Shambhala vision is to rectify that situation, not to make
the situation more autocratic or dictatorial. Leaders should be
more humble, and workers should be more proud, more arrogant
maybe. By the leaders' having humbleness and the workers' having more arrogance, there will be a meeting point somewhere.
Enlightened society can function that way, in the juxtaposition of
the two, in generations to come.

Often, the workers do not have enough arrogance. They feel
bad because they don't have enough money and possessions. The
leaders have too much of both. Even in many democracies, the
leaders are arrogant and proud—and sometimes deaf and dumb.
In 1980, members of the United States Congress hosted a luncheon for the head of my lineage of Tibetan Buddhism, His Holiness the Sixteenth Karmapa. I was invited to accompany him to
the Capitol, where I met a number of representatives and sena-
tors, including a senator who was supposed to be announcing his
candidacy for the presidency soon.

These people were completely deaf and dumb, completely
gone cuckoo! During the luncheon, they kept running out to vote
on the floor of the House or the Senate. Whenever a button would
light up on the wall, they had to run out and vote. I was quite
amazed that they could keep track of *anything*, because *they
weren't there*. It was amazing. You could actually tell who was the
highest and who was the lowest on the totem pole by how crazy
they were. The higher they were, the crazier. What does that say
about people in positions of power? The more power they get, the
crazier they become.

At lower levels of government, in my experience, it's quite
different. I also accompanied His Holiness when he visited the
city council of Boulder, Colorado, and those people were quite
smart and remarkable. If the council members met the members
of Congress, I wonder how they could communicate with each

102

other. The congressmen were *quite* amazing. And judging from that, imagine what a president would be like!

That seems to be the setting-sun idea of hierarchy. As you go higher, you don't even have to think. You just go bananas. By contrast, that should give you some idea of how to join heaven and earth. I would like to encourage the sitting practice of meditation, because I would like to see that what *we* do in the Shambhala world is definitely genuine. That genuineness has to come from you. I might present something genuine, but you might switch it into something else. Through the practice of meditation, you can make sure that the high standards of genuineness are kept properly and fully. At the same time, please enjoy yourselves.

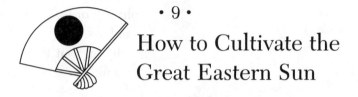

· 9 ·
How to Cultivate the Great Eastern Sun

Whether you have a good time or a bad time, you should feel sad and delighted at once. That is how to be a real, decent human being, and it is also connected with the Buddhist principle of longing, or devotion. Longing is the hunger for sacredness. When you begin to feel you're too much in the secular world, you long for a sacred world. Therefore, you feel sad, and you open yourself up that way. When you feel so sad and tender, that also brings ideas for how to uplift the rest of the world. Joining sadness and joy is the only mechanism that brings the vision of the Great Eastern Sun.

TO SUMMARIZE OUR DISCUSSION SO FAR: developing the ground of basic goodness is based on the idea of trust. Trust brings patience, freedom from laziness, and faith, which automatically lead to renunciation. At that point, we become quite clear as to what to accept and what to reject in order to care for others, and we begin to realize the merit of the sitting practice of meditation. Developing discrimination about what to accept and what to reject results in gentleness and also in realizing that the king of basic goodness joins heaven and earth together. Therefore, we find ourselves able to work with synchronizing mind and body together.

The fruition that we have now reached is connected with *know-how*—knowing how to go about practicing all of these lofty principles. We have to know how to act or manifest fully. We are not going to spend unnecessary time philosophizing or legitimizing the Shambhala principles. Time is short, and the situation is urgent. So we don't have time to discuss metaphysics, but we do have time to discuss know-how, how to do it. I would like to share that particular wisdom with all of you. In fact, I'm delighted to do so.

Working with yourself always involves a journey. As part of the journey, every one of us has to go through our own garbage. Some of it is real garbage, which should be discarded, and some of it is organic garbage, which can be recycled. One important point is that, when you're going through your garbage and sorting things out, you have to admit to yourself that you are not being a 100 percent ideal student. You improvise, you stick with your own neurosis sometimes, and you are cheating yourself, somewhat. As long as that is acknowledged, it is not regarded as absolutely evil at all. How much of the journey is genuine and how much of it is hypocritical is very hard to sort out. As long as you just keep doing it, it's fine. It only becomes problematic if you try to philosophize or rationalize the whole thing.

As far as the Shambhala principles are concerned, we don't believe in original sin. You are not fundamentally condemned. In fact, quite the opposite. Fundamentally, you are good. In spite of your hypocrisy, you are capable of being good, and what you express will be good as well. It will work out fine.

In discussing know-how, our larger theme is letting go: knowing how to let go, what to let go, and how to relax in our world.

In many cases, you've been given guidelines for how to relate with yourself and how to relate with others, but you haven't been given any guidelines for how to experience freedom. The expression of freedom has to come from you. Letting go is not being purely carefree in a sloppy style. You have to evaluate what portion of discipline should be maintained in the name of integrity and what portion of discipline should be relaxed. So letting go is still a training process. At the same time, it contains fruition-level logic.

The moment that we find ourselves as human beings—which takes place in the second after our birth—we realize we can cry and we can breathe because we are free from our mother's womb. From that time onward, we constantly exercise our individuality. We are no longer personally attached to our mother's umbilical cord, although there may still be emotional attachment, an emotional umbilical cord that still ties us to our mother. Nonetheless, as we grow, passing through our infancy, our teenage years, our youth, through middle age, and slowly into old age, we see ourselves stepping further and further away from our parents, further and further away from that kind of attachment. We are made into adult human beings purely because we are free from mother and father. We are made into individuals who can function independently. At the same time, we're encouraged to have a decent attitude toward others. All human beings share having a mother, a father, brothers and sisters. We should have a decent relationship with humanity.

The Shambhala society is very much concerned with what happens when we depart from the womb and regroup into the products of the womb, so to speak. We are asking people to remain clan-oriented, family-oriented. On the other hand, we're asking you *not* to hang on to the neurosis or the impetus that exists in being the child of somebody. We have to separate ourselves; at the same time, we have to come together in comradeship, working with human society. That is contradictory in itself, but it is at the same time full of wisdom.

If we look at the organization of society in the past—particularly among such ethnic groups as the Indian society, Jewish society, Polish society, Chinese society, Japanese society, and Tibetan society—we find that food was very important. The stove was very important. Cooking these days is too modernized. In the old days, people sat around the fire watching the pot boil, or watching the stove and putting firewood in it, sitting around in the kitchen. The stove is a very important part of civilization, a main sanctuary, actually. A lot of Americans probably have no idea about this, but we, as ethnic groups, understand.

How to be a family person, how to be a domestic person, how to relate with the wisdom of ancestral society, and how to worship it are not a product of neurosis or a lack of sophisticated modernization. People don't hang around the kitchen stove purely because their society is not modernized enough. Once you have electricity, you don't have to hang around the kitchen to keep warm or stoke the stove. Once you have central heating and air-conditioning, you don't have any central reference point anymore. It's interesting that the focus of family and livelihood has shifted so much. In the early days, that focus was based on the pretense of survival, but it was more than that. People developed their national family shrine around their mama and papa. The sacredness and the traditions that developed were handed down by your grandmother and grandfather. You received know-how from them; they taught you how to take care of yourself.

In the old days, before there were hospitals, naturally the grandmother came along and helped deliver the babies—knowing exactly what to do at every step. Then, after that, medical research incorporated the grandmother's wisdom, and hospitals and maternity wards developed. Grandmothers are no longer necessary, and they are probably parked in an old-age home. They don't have any role to play. The only thing for them to do is to come along and see that their grandchildren have been born and how nice they look. So the social system has changed that way.

When we talk about letting go, we are not talking about letting go of tradition. We are talking about letting go of the modern trappings that work against ideal human society. I am not particularly suggesting that we should develop the medieval old-fashioned style all over again, but I am talking about how things could be done better with some kind of effort, energy, and wisdom. One of the key points is to look at how people conduct themselves in traditional societies, such as the classical Jewish tradition, the classical Chinese tradition, and the classical Indian tradition. People in those societies have learned very simply how to choose a pot, how to cook in it, how to wash it, and how to put it away. It is the same principle as in the tradition of the Japanese tea ceremony. You might ask, "What's the big deal about learning how to use a pot, how to boil water in it, how to control the temperature of the fire, how to clean up after yourself? It's not going to change the presidential elections or anything like that." On the one hand, paying attention to those kinds of details is not particularly an earthshaking experience. On the other hand, it *might* be the key to the presidential elections.

Knowing how to relate with things simply—knowing how to handle a utensil, how to relate with water and fire, how to relate with vegetables—is normally regarded as something anybody can pick up on. But in today's society, people have a very difficult time knowing how to be natural and how to be precise. How to use an object properly and fully is complex. It's not necessarily complex on a scientific level. We're talking about the common-sense level, but common sense implies a lot of subtleties and sophistication as well.

MINDFULNESS AND AWARENESS

According to the Buddhist tradition, how you work with details is a twofold process. The first part is *the mindfulness of things as they are.* You have a pot or a teacup—whatever object you have. Mindfulness is how to work properly with those things. The second aspect is *awareness,* which is the totality of the situation. It is how your mindfulness is reflected in what you've done. Together, mindfulness and awareness are the first category or principle of letting go.

This may seem like a very simple, ordinary issue. Nonetheless, as far as the Shambhala wisdom is concerned, it is a very big issue: it is how to be a person, how to be a fully human being. Mindfulness first and awareness afterward bring what is known as *decency.* If you have mindfulness and awareness, you will be a decent person. Letting go does not mean getting wild or being a freak who can "let go" of everything. Rather, we are saying that, if you let yourself go fully and acknowledge your existence as you are, as a human being, then you will find yourself paying more attention to details, to the fullest extent possible. So from mindfulness and awareness, you become a decent person who knows how to relate with things as they are. That is the first category of letting go.

WINDHORSE

The second category is quite an interesting one. Having experienced letting go and having achieved a decent household, or a decent living situation, and a decent relationship with each other, we find that there is an uplifted quality that automatically exists in our lives. You could call it sacred existence, which is automatically created because of your mindfulness and awareness. We pay attention to details: we wash the dishes, we clean our room, we press our shirts, and we fold the sheets. When we pay attention to everything around us, the overall effect is upliftedness. The Shambhalian term for that is *windhorse*. The *wind* principle is very airy and powerful. *Horse* means that the energy is ridable. That particular airy and sophisticated energy, so clean and full of decency, can be ridden. You don't just have a bird flying by itself in the sky, but you have something to ride on. Such energy is fresh and exuberant but, at the same time, ridable. Therefore, it is known as windhorse.

Windhorse is also the idea of harnessing or riding on basic goodness. The wind of goodness is fresh and free from obstructions. Therefore, you can ride on it. So another term for riding on basic goodness is *riding on windhorse*. The experience of windhorse is that, because everything is so decent, so real, and so proper, therefore, it is workable. One begins to actually *experience* basic goodness, not on a philosophical level, but on a physical level. You begin to see how you as a human being can create basic goodness on the spot, fully, ideally.

Arising from that, we develop ideal heart. When we talk about "having heart," it usually refers to a military concept of bravery or gallantry, or it refers to a loving attitude within your family or domestic situation. But the Shambhala concept of having a heart is that, because you are able to ride on windhorse, everything is a projection of that uplifted decency. Having witnessed the full expression of basic goodness, we develop a real heart of genuineness.

JOINING TOGETHER SADNESS AND JOY TO BRING THE GREAT EASTERN SUN

The third category of letting go is *sadness and joy joined together*. Ordinarily, when you talk about feeling sad, it means that you are so hurt; you feel so bad. When you talk about feeling joyous, it means that you feel so excited and uplifted. Here you develop sadness and joy at once. You begin to feel tender— extremely tender and sad. When you fall in love for the first time, thinking about your lover, you have delightful ideas, but at the same time, you feel somewhat sad. It's not purely that your lover can't be with you or that your lover is long distant, but you feel tender even when you're together. On the spot, sharing the same room or the same bed, when you look at your lover, it feels wonderful. At the same time, it feels very touchy and sad. It is *wonderful*—in fact, it is ideal—that human emotions are expressed that way. When you feel sad, therefore, you feel great. Hot and cold, sweet and sour, at once, take place.

According to the Shambhala principles, you should feel that way with *everything* you do. Whether you have a good time or a bad time, you should feel sad and delighted at once. That is how to be a real, decent human being, and it is also connected with the Buddhist principle of longing, or devotion. Longing is the hunger for sacredness. When you begin to feel you're too much in the secular world, you long for a sacred world. Therefore, you feel sad, and you open yourself up that way. When you feel so sad and tender, that also brings ideas for how to uplift the rest of the world. Joining sadness and joy is the only mechanism that brings the vision of the Great Eastern Sun.

The Great Eastern Sun has three categories. From the experience of the simultaneity of sadness and joy, we *radiate peaceful confidence*, which is the first quality of the Great Eastern Sun. Second is *illuminating the way of discipline*, which is realizing what to accept and what to reject, as we discussed before. That aspect of the Great Eastern Sun is like turning on the light. If you are standing in the middle of a dark room and you have no idea what's around you, when you switch on the light, you will know what to accept and reject. The third quality is becoming the *eternal ruler of the three worlds*, or conquering the three worlds. Having developed a sad and joyous situation, seeing what to accept and what to reject, therefore, you feel a sense of joy and achievement. This is conquering the threefold world, which, roughly speaking, corresponds to the heaven, earth, and man, or human, principles.

Conquering here is very personal. It is related to one's attitude toward oneself and one's world when one begins to see the Great Eastern Sun. You could say that, when you switch on the light, it conquers your room because there's no darkness left. Conquering here is not the concept of a battle. It's just switching on the light. That is the synopsis, so to speak, of the qualities of the Great Eastern Sun.

How to cultivate the Great Eastern Sun, as we discussed already, comes from joy and sadness put together, which might be something like sweet-and-sour pork.

STUDENT: Could you say something about what you mean by heaven and earth?

DORJE DRADUL OF MUKPO: What do you think it could be? Do you have any ideas?

STUDENT: I think I can understand it when you talk in terms of synchronizing body and mind.

DORJE DRADUL OF MUKPO: But what about heaven and earth themselves? What's earth?

STUDENT: Well, that's where I'm sitting.

DORJE DRADUL OF MUKPO: Good. From that, you can tell what heaven is. It's our reference point with each other.

STUDENT: But that sounds like being in the middle of a sandwich.

DORJE DRADUL OF MUKPO: Well, maybe you *are* in a sandwich. We're always sandwiched because we have a past, we have a present, and we have a future. We are sandwiched by our father, our mother, our child. Even timewise, we are sandwiched. We are sandwiched between breakfast, lunch, and dinner.

Heaven is anything that is spacious. It includes your lofty ideas, your beliefs, your metaphysics, your wishes, your desires. It is anything you hold as sacred, anything you might put in your safe-deposit box: your jewelry, your birth certificate, your college diploma. Earth is related with your personal existence, your car keys, the key to your apartment, money in your wallet, your husband, your wife, your groceries for the night or for the rest of the week. So heaven is the lofty principle, and earth is what you actually *have* in your refrigerator or your bank account.

Joining them together is challenging. If you think in terms of how a nation might join heaven and earth together, it gets quite complicated. But if you begin with yourself and how you relate personally to joining heaven and earth, that's quite simple and domestic. You might think that your personal heaven and earth are not sacred enough to be joined together. But in the Shambhala world, we have fundamental appreciation and respect for whatever we do. Every act is a sacred act. With that inspiration, we regard every experience in our life as sacred as well. Therefore, we can join heaven and earth together. It could be as mundane as going to the supermarket to buy toilet tissue. You bring it home, then you use it, and you flush it down the toilet. You are joining heaven and earth together. When you buy it, you have heaven. When you use it, you have earth. You join them together, and it's very beautiful. You can accomplish the whole thing.

We have reached a natural conclusion. From the discovery of basic goodness comes renunciation, and out of that, daring develops. Finally, we can appreciate and enjoy our individual existence as warriors. There is natural pride involved in leading life and appreciating existence as a good Shambhala person.

My family and I have been trying to establish the Shambhala training for quite a number of years. Establishing a firm ground is difficult, but once the ground is established, then new students find their way, quite easily. The hard work of the first students put together with the aspirations of newer students fulfills the purpose of the work. First you have the sky; then the sun rises out of that. The two are complementary. When sky and sun meet together, the Great Eastern Sun can manifest and shine.

The Great Eastern Sun is not realized purely because of philosophy or the existence of some organization. It is your individual participation that becomes wonderfully powerful and encourages us all. I personally have taken a vow to work with all of you and furthermore with the rest of the world. We can always trust in and fearlessly appreciate the Great Eastern Sun. We should take a vow not to use it for our personal achievement at all. If we do that, we will decline.

I appreciate sharing this teaching with you, and I hope that you can manifest yourselves further. The beauty and the glory of the warrior students prove that what we are doing is absolutely the right thing to do, and wonderful. Please be a warrior, as long as there is life, which will be several billion years. Welcome to the Great Eastern Sun vision.

PART THREE

JUST

· 10 ·

Blamelessness · How to Love Yourself

A lot of problems come from self-hatred. Let us let go of that; let us let it go away. Let us be as real people. Let us be genuine people who don't require doctors, medicine, aspirin, codeine, all the rest of it. Let us be just basic human beings.

See the beautiful deer. They have no one to rule them, but they frolic in the meadow as if they had a deerkeeper. They are so clean; they have such head and shoulders; they are beautifully horned. The deer, the fox, the jackal—all have their own beauty in being themselves. Nobody is taking care of them.

MY NAME IS LORD MUKPO OF TIBET. I know that the American revolutionary world has rejected the king, along with the lords. But I'm afraid that these lords and ladies will come back again and again. Particularly, in connection with Shambhala vision, this lord is returning to the United States of America—coming not from Great Britain but from Tibet.

Maybe we should discuss the word *lord*, which has several different meanings. A lord could be a person who enslaves others, a person who rules others, or a person who actually promotes lordship in others. I am the third type of lord. We are all lords or ladies, one way or another. My name is Lord Mukpo, and I'm proud of that. I have done my duty, as my duty has called for me to do. I have never tired of performing my duty, and one of my duties is to present the Shambhala principles to you.

The Shambhala message is not a very complicated one: it is simply that the human condition can be worked out, or we might say, conditions of neurosis can be overcome. That is the essence. It may not be all that different from what you have heard before, except that a lord is presenting this to you. In this case, being a lord is the same as being a sentient being. This particular lord has been subject to simple living, including almost animal-realm situations, and he has worked his way through them. This lord has seen the problems of human society, and he has understood them. All of you have been to school, where you have gone through a process of learning and discipline, and you have been punished and praised by your schoolmasters and schoolmistresses. This lord has gone through the same thing.

The point of Shambhala vision is to benefit others. We are not going to be simply strong, self-made individuals. You might think that, when you become a lord, you are going to employ servants. "I'm going to project my power onto others to subjugate them. They're going to listen to what I have to say, and my wishes and commands will be carried out." In this case, it is just the opposite. Lordship is just like loving someone for the first time in your life or falling in love with someone. We are talking about that kind of sympathy and gentleness. That is the essence of lordship.

You are inquisitive enough to listen to the sound of someone's voice. You are inquisitive enough to look at somebody's face. You are inquisitive enough to smell somebody's body. You are inquisitive enough to touch someone's body. I am not particularly presenting a pornographic description of Shambhala vision. But passion has been undermined so much, particularly by religiosity, by just a simple remark like "Sex is bad." We are not saying here that sex is the best, either. Rather, we are talking about human nature and the human virtue, or goodness, of helping others. How to help others, how to like somebody, or how to love somebody are often so mixed up. We hear dreadful stories, such as the stories about priests making it with their parishioners. There is all that garbage that goes on, all those human stories. We might discuss warped love later, but here we are talking about fresh love. Our subject matter is benefiting others, working for others. To work for others, we have to work on ourselves. We have to love ourselves. We have to be gentle with ourselves. That is the main point: as human beings, we need to develop gentleness, which is genuineness.

Along with that comes a sense of surrendering and a feeling of revulsion and disgust toward the world. We're not talking about seeing the world through rose-tinted glass or purely thinking that the world is beautiful. First, help yourself. Develop a sense of healthiness and a sense of *me helping others*. "This person, Joe Schmidt, is a great helper of others." Then you see the ugliness— people's confusion and their resentment and aggression toward the world. Often, someone may try to convert you to his or her aggressive system of thinking. The main point is not to join that person. That is very important and quite straightforward. (Maybe someone from California will have a problem understanding that, but certainly those from New York will have no difficulty with this idea.)

The second point is to trust in your heart, which is very, very simple. Trust in your heart. How? Why? When? Which heart? How do you do that? You might ask all those questions. The answer is simply *because you are here*. How do you know that the ceiling won't drop on your head? Or that the floor won't give way, so that you end up in the basement? Trust. Trust starts from realiz-

119

ing that there are trillions of worthwhile people who want to connect with Shambhala vision and with basic goodness. Therefore, you develop a sense of warriorship, which is free from cowardice, or nervousness as it is commonly known in America. But the actual, technical term is *cowardice*. This has nothing to do with milk, of course. *Cow*-ard, *cow*-ard, and *cow*-ard. In fact, the cow-ard is the opposite of the cow-cow. This cow does not even give milk. It is too cowardly to give milk; it is completely dry and shaking.

The Tibetan word for warrior is *pawo*. *Pa* means "ignoring the challenger" or "ignoring the other's challenge." *Wo* makes it a noun. So the warrior is one who does not engage others' sense of aggression. When there's no aggression, trust takes place. Out of that genuine sense of warriorship comes joy. For the first time in your life, you feel at ease. "Goodness gracious! Why on earth have I been driving myself mad by being petrified by all these things around me? And how has it happened that I can finally relax?" Whew. Tremendous relaxation, which comes with a tremendous smile. It comes with natural head and shoulders.

When you relax in the ordinary sense, it is like when the flight attendant on an airplane says, "The captain has turned the SEAT BELT sign off now. You can move around the cabin, and we're going to serve you a drink and a meal and show you a movie." That's inviting you to be floppy. You can sit back, watch a movie, have a drink, and eat good food. Actually, it's usually bad food. The conventional sense of relaxation might also be that you feel as though you're about to vomit and then you relieve that feeling with a big burp. On the airplane, if you feel sick to your stomach, the flight attendant might say, "Go ahead. We don't mind if you throw up. We'll clean up after you." No head and shoulders. With good head and shoulders, you are not going to vomit, belch, or burp, but you *are* going to be yourself. "I am Joe Schmidt." "I am Jane Doe." "I am Lodrö Dorje." "I am Ösel Tendzin." "I am

Diana Mukpo." "I am Chögyam Trungpa Mukpo."[1] Taking pride in your existence with good head and shoulders is the antidote to sickness, the trick to antiflop, and that is the ground of our discussion.

The last point I'd like to discuss is blamelessness. Usually, when things go wrong, we come up with an excuse. "Why did you kill the president?" You come up with a logical reason, so that you are not to blame. "Poor me. I had to assassinate the president because I'm psychotic." Or you think of something else that caused you to do this. To overcome that approach, true blamelessness is very important. Whether you are a Buddhist or a Shambhala practitioner, when you don't keep up with your meditation practice, you begin to cook up all sorts of logics. "The reason I'm not practicing my Shambhala discipline or my Buddhist discipline is that my marriage has fallen apart." "I've been sick." "I couldn't sleep." "I have no money." Blah, blah, blah. The point here is to develop real blamelessness rather than coming up with such logical excuses—which might even give you a reason to sue others. (We have a problem of having too many lawyers in this country.)

The point here is to make ourselves tight and disciplined. We don't give in to any religious, metaphysical, or psychological problems. We just maintain ourselves as we are. We can be simply what we are. That is the basic point. You have to take responsibility. It is your duty. You are not fundamentally sick. Everybody has a duty, and you do pretty well as yourself, as what you are. You could help a lot of people. That's what we're talking about.

I don't want to play down the colorfulness of the early poems

---

1. After using two common anonymous names as examples, the author uses the names of several students present in the audience when he gave this talk. Lodrö Dorje was the Dorje Loppon, or the head of practice and study for Vajradhatu, the main Buddhist organization founded by Chögyam Trungpa. Ösel Tendzin was the Vajra Regent, the author's Buddhist heir. Diana Mukpo was the author's wife. And of course, the last-named person is the author himself.

of my friend Allen Ginsberg, but when he made poetry out of his reaction to the Vietnam War and other problems that America faced, he could have been contributing to the problems. The ground of blamelessness is connecting with things as they are, the simple, clean-cut level, definitely the clean-cut level of things as they are. If you see something wrong, say it. You don't have to say it in a pejorative or negative sense at all. Just say it and do something about it. Talk to your friends. Tell them: let us not do *this*, let us do *that*. In fact, every one of you has tremendous power. You don't have to be the president of the United States, particularly. You can be your own king or queen.

Blamelessness is a very simple point. Blame doesn't come from one's partners or friends. Taking blame onto yourself means that it is *yours*. In other words, when you're outside and you shout something, if it bounces off a rock, then the rock says, "ai, ai, ai, ai." But you don't blame the rock. You blame yourself, because *you* said "ai, ai, ai, ai." You're in an echo chamber, so you blame the echo*er* rather than the echo itself. Therefore, there is hope; there is hope of reducing blame.

When you are afraid of something, it might be a fear of darkness, a fear of knives, a fear of guns, or of anything. You can't just have fear without fear *of* something. So what is that other? Who is the other? That's *yourself*. There is a story about a man who's locked in a room. He's sitting in that room, a big room with lots of space and lots of possibilities of noise bouncing back. Things are getting cold and dark and darker. He hears something. So he says, "Who dat?" When there is no response, he says, "Who dat who said, 'Who dat?'?" And then he says, "Who dat who said, 'Who dat?' when I said, 'Who dat?'?" The antidote to that echo chamber is to make friends with yourself.

Give yourself a break. That doesn't mean to say that you should drive to the closest bar and have lots to drink or go to a movie. Just enjoy the day, your normal existence. Allow yourself to sit in your home or take a drive into the mountains. Park your car somewhere; just sit; just be. It sounds very simplistic, but it has a lot of magic. You begin to pick up on clouds, sunshine and weather, the mountains, your past, your chatter with your grandmother and your grandfather, your own mother, your own father. You begin to pick up on a lot of things. Just let them pass like the chatter of a brook as it hits the rocks. We have to give ourselves some time to be.

We've been clouded by going to school, looking for a job—our lives are cluttered by all sorts of things. Your friends want you to come have a drink with them, which you don't want to do. Life is crowded with all sorts of garbage. In themselves, those things aren't garbage, but they're cumbersome when they get in the way of how to relax, how to be, how to trust, how to be a warrior. We've missed so many possibilities for that, but there are so many more possibilities that we can catch. We have to learn to be kinder to ourselves, much more kind. Smile a lot, although nobody is watching you smile. Listen to your own brook, echoing yourself. You can do a good job.

In the sitting practice of meditation, when you begin to be still, hundreds of thousands, millions, and billions of thoughts will go through your mind. But they just pass through, and only the worthy ones leave their fish eggs behind. We have to leave ourselves some time to be. You're not going to see the Shambhala vision, you're not even going to survive, by not leaving yourself a minute to be, a minute to smile. If you don't grant yourself a good time, you're not going to get any Shambhala wisdom, even if you're at the top of your class technically speaking. Please, I beg you, please, give yourself a good time. ⸺

This doesn't mean that you have to go to an expensive clothing store to buy three-thousand-dollar suits. You don't have to go to the most expensive restaurant to eat. For that matter, you don't have to go to a bar and get drunk. The way to give yourself a good time is to be gentle with yourself. A lot of problems come from self-hatred. Let us let go of that; let us let it go away. Let us *be* as real people. Let us be genuine people who don't require doctors, medicine, aspirin, codeine, all the rest of it. Let us be just basic human beings.

See the beautiful deer. They have no one to rule them, but they frolic in the meadow as if they had a deerkeeper. They are so clean; they have such head and shoulders; they are beautifully horned. The deer, the fox, the jackal—all have their own beauty in being themselves. Nobody is taking care of them.

I'm somewhat appalled that we can't do that for ourselves. On the other hand, it is a human condition that has been handed down through the generations. Now is the time for that to end. Now is the time of hope for us. The wisdom of the East comes to the West. The Shambhala teaching is here right now, completely pure and undiluted by anybody at all. You are so fortunate, if I may say so, on behalf of my forebears and grandparents and myself. It is wonderful that you have this opportunity. Please don't waste your time. Every minute is important. Nonetheless, have a good sleep, and don't work while you're asleep!

I

First it swells and goes where it will,
Isn't this a river?
It rises in the East and sets in the West,
Isn't this the moon?

II

Never setting,
Isn't this the Great Eastern Sun?
Whether it exists or not,
It is the Shambhala kingdom.

III

Love that is free from hesitation
And passion that is free from laziness
Can join East and West.
Then, South and North also arise.
You arise as the king of the whole world.
You can join both heaven and earth.

IV

Being without fear, you create fear.
The renown of fear cannot be feared.
When through fear you examine yourself,
You trample on the egg of fear.

These four untitled poems were written on the same day that the talk "Blamelessness" was given.

· 11 ·

Attaining the Higher Realms

You can help the world. You, you, you, you, and you—all of you—can help the world. You know what the problems are. You know the difficulties. Let us do something. Let us not chicken out. Let us actually do it properly. Please, please, please! We are trying to reach the higher realms and help others to do so, instead of being stuck in the hell realm, the hungry ghost realm, and the animal realm—which are the other alternatives, the lower realms. Let's do it. Please think about that. I wish that you would all take a personal vow to help others who are going through such turmoil.

BLAMELESSNESS, or being without blame, comes from being daring. You might say, "How dare you call me Joe Schmidt? How *dare* you? *How dare* you?" When you say that, you automatically raise your head and shoulders. If you look at yourself in the mirror when you say, "How dare you?" you will see that. So this kind of daring is human upliftedness.

Daring is very direct, but at the same time, it's somewhat difficult to attain, because, in many cases, we don't like ourselves.

We feel that we aren't equipped with everything that we should have, so we don't feel very good about ourselves. In fact, we feel that we have a lot of problems. We consider some of those things to be private matters. "I can't have an orgasm," or "I acted impulsively. I shouted at somebody when I didn't need to." There are a lot of situations where we feel inadequate, bad, or strange. The way to overcome all of that is to have a loving attitude toward yourself.

When you pay attention or you want to hear what someone is saying, you sit or stand upright. Interestingly enough, the ears make head and shoulders: if somebody says something that you have to strain to hear, you perk up your ears to listen. That is precisely the image of Deer Park, which is His Holiness Karmapa's logo. Two deer are sitting on either side of the wheel of *dharma*, which represents the proclamation of the Buddhist teachings, trying to listen to the Karmapa teaching. It's as if they were saying, "What did he say? What's it all about?" The same is true in many of the traditional *thangkas,* or paintings, of Milarepa, a great Tibetan Buddhist saint who wrote many beautiful songs of meditative realization. He is often shown cupping his right hand over his ear, listening to himself singing his own song. He's cupping his hand to his ear so that he can hear his own voice singing

the melody and the words of the song. Listening is a sense of personal inquisitiveness, which brings a sense of satisfaction. At least you can hear the music!

We have to help others who cannot hear. We can help them by providing a sense of joy. To those who feel aggression toward the world, we can say, "Experiencing the world is not all that bad, my dear friend. This world is not all that terrorized by passion, aggression, or ignorance." When you make a new friend who has never heard of such a thing as Shambhala wisdom or buddha-dharma, the teachings of the Buddha, you might invite him or her to join you in a cup of coffee or some good scotch. Then you can sit back together and listen to this world. In that way, you can share the experience that the world is workable. It's not all *that* bad at all. You might find that the alcohol provides possibilities to share the space together. The next day, when your friend wakes up, they may have a hangover and they may go back to their depressed world. Still, it's better that your friend have the hangover.

We're trying to cheer up the rest of the world—including ourselves. As you practice and come to understand the Shambhala teachings, some genuineness takes place. You begin to see that snow is actually much whiter, winter is so beautiful, and summer is fabulous. I have created dharma art installations that demonstrate those sorts of possibilities.[1] It is possible to cheer up. Good heavens! Please believe me. It is possible to cheer up in all sorts of different ways, and it is absolutely possible to cheer up the world.

At this point, the world is depressed. That is our main con-

1. *Dharma art* is a term coined by the author to refer to art that is based on nonaggression and that expresses the basic dharma, or truth, of things as they are. *Dharma Art*, a book presenting the author's views on art, was published in 1996 by Shambhala Publications. The installations he refers to here were a series of rooms that embodied different qualities and aspects of life and utilized interesting arrangements of colors, furniture, and objects, often with provocative flower arrangements in their midst.

cern. Sometimes the world has been uplifted in a negative way, such as during the Vietnam War or during the two world wars. People had something to cheer them up, because they had a proper enemy: "The Germans have a big gun, but on the other hand, ours might be better." But how are we going to cheer up when there's no enemy? What if the economy becomes depressed? The point is that it is up to you individually. You have to cheer yourselves up, to begin with. Charity begins at home, as they say. Then others are no longer a nuisance, and the world around you is a good world, the best world. It becomes your partner, your friend. Even if your car runs into another car and makes a big dent, that might provide a topic of conversation. First, ARRRRR! Then, it may become a joke, quite funny. Then, you can make friends. "Where do you live? Come for dinner. Come for a drink." It's possible. Particularly in the United States of America, those possibilities exist.

The key to blamelessness is nonaggression, definitely. When you're angry, you become extremely intelligent. You say, "This happened because of that and that and that." Or you say, "He did this, and he did that," or, "She did this, and she did that, and therefore, this happened." Aggression has a tendency to become *so* intelligent, and it begins to spread and split into further levels of aggression. When you're really angry and aggressive, there is a tendency to smear the excrement of aggression on everybody. That's why the Shambhala vision of nonaggression is so important. Whenever you're tempted to blame something on someone else, saying, "This happened because of that," or, "That has happened because of this," just come back to your oneness. The Shambhala principle of wholeness is like a Ming vase that has no cracks in it. It holds together majestically as a Ming vase with its intricate designs. Try to maintain that sense of being. When there is ARRRRR!—think of the Ming vase. And you could think of me, too!

Appreciating your perceptions is the next topic. The way your hair is done, the way your clothes are worn, the way you handle all the details of your life have a lot to do with the basic sense of daring. You don't have to buy the most expensive suit from Brooks Brothers. Simply keep yourself neat and tidy, whatever you wear. And when you look at yourself, take pride in yourself. That kind of pride is not regarded as arrogance at all. Just be a good lady, a good gentleman. Take pride in yourself. Even though you might be wearing just a sheet or a loincloth, still, you can be elegant. I don't quite mean that literally, but there are such possibilities. Look at yourself. You are fantastic; you look so good. You are capable. You *do* have the goodness that we've been discussing.

The key to daring is your state of mind. When there's no aggression, there is natural passion—the passion to be, the passion to beautify yourself, the passion to look good, the passion to hold up your head and shoulders. *Head and shoulders* means, in this case, the basic elegance of enlightenment, as the Buddha exemplified. If you want to know what I'm talking about, you might look at some of the statues of the *lohans*, who were Buddhist saints and great practitioners of meditation. You can see their posture of good head and shoulders.

You can achieve that, not only for yourself, but you can help others to uplift themselves. If you have a child or a little brother or sister who thrives on being a hunchback when he or she eats—hunching over and making a lot of noises while shoveling in the food—you can correct the child's behavior. "John, sit up." "Joanne, sit up." "Let's eat a nice, elegant dinner together." That doesn't mean you have to go out and buy the best Wedgwood china, but you can still have a beautiful meal, nicely presented, properly eaten, properly drunk.

The goal of the Shambhala teachings is to uplift human conditions. Ever since the creation of the notion of a republic and the creation of the notion of individualism, leadership has gone down-

hill. Our leaders—kings and queens, presidents and prime ministers—have failed us. Let us have a new king, a good queen, a good
prime minister. Let us have good head and shoulders. Let us eat
properly at our dining room tables; let us drink properly; and let
us not overindulge. The rich are the worst offenders in this part
of the world, because they can afford to drink from sunrise to

sunset, but at the end of it all, they still go downhill, with no notion of human dignity, no notion of daring, no notion of goodness at all. I suppose we could call that some kind of magic bad joke.

You are the vanguard of human society. We talk about the dark age and how the world is going downhill. The world might destroy itself, but *not quite yet.* You are the vanguard to uplift your society—to begin with, your parents, your friends. There is such a thing as the Shambhala principle of upliftedness. It is the simple appreciation of the world, the appreciation of the sunrise, and also the appreciation that the one dot, one thought, does exist. When somebody is choking or about to throw up, that person only thinks one thought, just one thought. And that's a good thought! It cuts all the rest of the thoughts. I hope you understand.

From that one good thought, a person can start to eat properly, work properly, sleep properly, sit properly. And from that, you can understand and attain the higher realms. The higher realms are the realm of the gods; the realm of the demigods, or the jealous gods; and the human realm. The realm of the gods, by the way, doesn't mean the realm of Jehovah, *the* God, but just godliness. The realm of the jealous gods is consumed with achievement and competition. It is the realm of energy, competence, and power. The human realm, very simply, is the realm where we can be proper human beings. Traditionally, it is necessary to attain these states of mind or states of existence and to transcend the horrific pain of the lower realms before you can attain ultimate freedom or enlightenment.

I'm quite desperate. A lot of other teachers must have experienced this desperation. I am so desperate. You can help the world. You, you, you, you, and you—all of you—can help the world. You know what the problems are. You know the difficulties. Let us do something. Let us not chicken out. Let us actually do it properly. Please, please, please! We are trying to reach the higher realms and help others to do so, instead of being stuck in the hell realm, the hungry ghost realm, and the animal realm—which are the other alternatives, the lower realms. Let's do it. Please think about that. I wish that you would all take a personal vow to help others who are going through such turmoil. People often say that it's too difficult to work with others. It's impossible to help them. But that's not true. It has been done. Look at yourselves. You are all uplifted people. You are part of the higher realms. Some of you might question that about yourselves, but it's not a real question. It's just a thought.

Shambhala vision applies to people of any faith, not just people who believe in Buddhism. Anyone can benefit from the Shambhala training and Shambhala vision, without its undermining their faith or their relationship with their minister, their priest, their bishop, their pope, whatever religious leaders they may follow. The Shambhala vision does not distinguish a Buddhist from a Catholic, a Protestant, a Jew, a Moslem, a Hindu. That's why we call it the Shambhala *kingdom.* A kingdom should have lots of different spiritual disciplines in it. That's why we are here.

We may talk about elegance and beauty and such highfalutin stuff as kingship. But we are fundamentally talking about settling down and having a home. Maybe you should get married. Find out about taking care of a child, having a husband or wife, having a home. It will change your entire life! Go look for a mate, have a baby, have a beautiful home, whatever you can afford. You might marry a rich man or woman, but even if you don't, you can make your home beautiful. The point is that we're talking about *life.* Of course, not every Shambhalian has to get married. The main point is not feeding one's own ego or one's self-deception.

People in the past—including even Marx, Lenin, and Mao Tse-tung—tried to figure out how people could live together in society. I've read some very interesting books by people who worked *so* hard for the benefit of others. I would recommend the writings on Quakerism and also the Rudolph Steiner philosophy. Just make sure that you don't get carried away with them. They may only be about 40 percent trustworthy, but still, they're extremely good. Those early pioneers were really trying to explore Shambhala-type possibilities. Unfortunately, they lacked a spiritual discipline such as the sitting practice of meditation, which the buddhadharma offers. So they didn't know precisely how to do it, but nevertheless, I think it would be valuable to study the literature of the Quakers and the Steiner school. They weren't like Hitler, Mussolini, or Mao Tse-tung. They were real human people. Well, of course, they were human! I mean here that they were human-concerned people, concerned about others. They didn't want to rule the world. They simply wanted to experience the reality of the world and to present it to others.

For instance, Rudolph Steiner thought that children shouldn't see any sharp corners, so in the educational system that he developed, columns and picture frames were always rounded. That might be slightly crazy. But generally, we should be appreciative of people who have put so much energy into understanding the world, so that we can finally have Shambhala vision.

Many people have tried their best to present Shambhala possibilities. We can't look down on them and say how stupid and uninspired they were. Each one of those people was a fantastic individual. For instance, George Fox, the Quaker who lived in the 1600s, in his own way introduced the notion of meditation. In those days, you couldn't get married without saying a prayer. But George Fox simply said, "There is not going to be any prayer. The bride and bridegroom are going to sit in silence and get married in that silence." Isn't that revolutionary, especially for that time in history?

It would be worth investigating further the origins of Shambhala vision in the European traditions. It would be good to conduct a study of Western historical figures who tried to achieve the

Shambhala vision of enlightened society. Some of you might have a tendency to be uppity and look down on the past, which shouldn't really happen at all. People of the past have not just achieved some simple little thing. They have contributed so much wisdom to the world. We should pay tribute to those people of the past and appreciate them as our ancestors.

That is the fruition or the conclusion of our discussion. However, warriors of the Great Eastern Sun never say good night. We always say good morning no matter what time of day it is, because we are not connected with the setting sun at all. We always say good morning because the Great Eastern Sun always shines. *Great* means that you are not infected by ignorance. *East* is where things always begin. The sun always rises in the east. And *Sun* is all-pervasive power and strength, which illuminate your responsibility as well as your genuineness. Genuineness always shines through, like the sun. We've already said quite a lot about *good,* and *morning* I don't have to explain. It is always morning.

The Big No

You cannot destroy life. You cannot by any means, for any religious, spiritual, or metaphysical reasons, step on an ant or kill your mosquitoes—at all. That is Buddhism. That is Shambhala. You have to respect everybody. You cannot make a random judgment on that at all. That is the rule of the king of Shambhala, and that is the Big No. You can't act on your desires alone. You have to contemplate the details of what needs to be removed and what needs to be cultivated.

OUR TOPIC IS DECENCY. Decency here is not in contrast to the indecency of, say, wearing two different-colored socks or not having your zipper done up. We are talking about decency as something more profound to be realized and understood. The first part of decency is what is called modesty, which here is the absence of arrogance. The second part of decency is being *so* kind and wise, but without laying your trip on others.

Decency means never being tired or made haggard by others. There's always some enjoyment in dealing with the world, whether you are dealing with people, with other sentient beings, or even with inanimate objects. You could be dealing with your garden; it could be your horse; it could be your dog, your cat, or your stove. No matter what you are doing, the sense of decency is being absolutely on the spot, without falling to the level of uncaring and crudeness.

Finally, decency is being loyal to others, loyal to the most intimate experiences that you've shared with others, and it is having loyalty to the principle of Shambhala vision. I would like to encourage that enormously. The Shambhala *training* is just an educational system, and we are not asking for your loyalty to that, particularly. You can hold on to being a Freudian or a Jungian, or to whatever philosophy you hold. Nonetheless, you should also hold your loyalty to Shambhala vision. That loyalty is twofold. Quite simply, it is a commitment to (1) working gently with yourself and (2) being kind to others. When those two concur, there's no alternative, no other way but to develop enlightened society. So enlightened society is quite an important part of our work and our vision. Enlightened society is pragmatic: it comes from trust, faith, and the genuine experience of reality. At the same time, it requires greater and further vision to propagate this vision to other human beings, to bring them into this society.

The next aspect of decency is being free from trickery, free from the tricks we play on ourselves or on each other to maintain our basic existence. When we're having trouble maintaining our ground or our selves, we play all kinds of tricks. For example, you invite a potential employee to dinner so that you can seduce him or her with an offer, saying, "Look, I can offer you this great job and all this money. Please come work for me and build my ego up for me. Please do." Trickery brings hope and fear. You're so tempted; at the same time, you're so afraid.

According to the Shambhala teachings, the way to be free from that self-deception is to appreciate the phenomenal world, free from hope and fear: the sun and the moon, the clouds and the bright blue sky—or the gray sky. Pine trees and rocks, gardens and green grasses—or the gray grasses of the snow. Buildings that are tumbling down, buildings that are perfectly erected. House-wives coming in and out of shops. People with briefcases walking in and out of their offices. The taxi drivers' pole providing a meet-ing point for the driver and the passenger. Flags flying on a metal rod jingle as their grommets hit the pole. The world is full of all sorts of things. In fact, I feel that I don't have to actually retell you *your* world. You already know it.

In the case of *my* world, it used to be that, in my country, Tibet, when we woke up in the morning, we could smell the wood burning as breakfast was being cooked. We could smell butter and tea being churned for our morning drink. In the monastery where I lived, in the early morning, I might see an attendant coming in to clean my living quarters, and I would hear the devotees offer-ing their prayers to the shrines. After the morning chants, we would have a hearty breakfast, very hearty. I think that, quite pos-sibly, it was more than six times heartier than an American break-fast, even huevos rancheros.

After our big breakfast, we Tibetans would go about our busi-ness. Some of us would go out journeying to sell things. If you were a farmer, you would take care of your animals. If you were an official, your business might include punishing a criminal by beating them with a cane. Traditionally, that was the punishment for someone who tried to hunt deer on your land. That crime required three canes. The person had both hands tied up behind them so that the shoulder sockets would begin to turn inward, which was quite painful. Those punishments were laid down by tradition, which now the Chinese communists call "the feudalism of Tibet." Frankly, I don't see why the Tibetans were regarded as the worst of the worst by the Chinese regime. *Their* feudalism was absolutely worse and terrifying. At the Chinese court, for instance, there might be ten sweepers to clean the courtyard. There would be five whippers assigned to whip the sweepers whenever they took time off. If a sweeper stopped sweeping, they would be whipped with a particular kind of whip that draws blood.

Nonetheless, that is not particularly our concern here in the West. We're not, by any means, expecting that kind of ignorance to be propagated here at all. The closest thing to whipping and sweeping in our world is typing letters and vacuum cleaning. When you are employed in an office and you have a boss who tells you what to do, it is somewhat like being one of those sweepers in the courtyard. In a lot of cases, you find that you're smarter than your boss. Just like the sweepers, you would like to take a break now and then, or you *have* to take a break. Occasionally, your computer breaks down, or your printer runs out of ink. You might like to take your lunch break, you wish some good coffee had been made, or you have a sudden desire for a sandwich. All those things are natural phenomena.

Why am I saying all this? Because we have to realize that we live in a society: we *have* society, and we *are* society. Every one of you is part of society. Maybe some of you don't work in the way that I just described. Maybe you have enough money to spend a lot of time skiing, swimming, diving, or motor-scooting. There are all kinds of possible lifestyles, but as far as the majority is concerned, the system of livelihood is based on going to work, having a regular job.

Sometimes we have a tendency to ignore problems in the world, by saying, "Well, that's *their* problem." Sometimes we have a tendency to get too close to situations. We are so involved with women's liberation, men's liberation, saving the Hopis, helping the Tibetans, all kinds of things like that. On the whole—beyond your own personal discipline, the practice of meditation, and working with your own mind—I'm trying to look at how we can actually relate with the world at large and how we can help this particular world. I would be so delighted to hear your ideas and approaches to being of service to the world, without creating what is known as the setting sun. That includes your own setting sun.

Occasionally watching a football game or an interesting movie on television is fine, but if you're completely glued to the set, it becomes setting sun. Taking a holiday at the seaside, staying in a hotel, appreciating the sand, the sunshine, the water—even waterskiing—in the proper season is lovely. But if you become a fanatic, making a cult out of worshiping the sun and wanting to be a beachboy for the rest of your life, then you are in the setting sun. Reading books, being interested in scholarship, and appreciating the knowledge that has been presented to us and worked for by our ancestors—that's all fine. People have worked very hard for us. But if you intellectualize everything, you don't even know how to cook a boiled egg. You're so into your bookie that you don't even hear the water boiling on the stove. While it's boiling, you're still stuck in your book, glued to it. That is the setting sun.

The antidote to a setting-sun mentality is to be free from deception. In connection with that, I'd like to tell you about the Big No, which is different than just saying no to our little habits, such as scratching yourself like a dog. When human beings scratch themselves, we try to do it in a slightly more sophisticated way, but we're still scratching. The ordinary Shambhala type of no applies to things like scratching—or not scratching—yourself or keeping your hair brushed. That no brings a sense of discipline rather than constantly negating you. In fact, it's a *yes*, the biggest yes. It is part of learning how to be human, as opposed to how to be an animal. The Big No is a whole different level of no.

The Big No arose some time ago when I was together with my vajra regent[1] and several students at the Kalapa Court, my

1. The Vajra Regent, Ösel Tendzin, was the American student (born Thomas Rich) who was appointed by Chögyam Trungpa in 1976 as his dharma heir, or the heir to

house. When the Big No came out, I had found that everybody was indulging in their world too much. I had to say No. So I crashed my arm and fist down on my coffee table, and I broke it. I put a dent in it. Then I painted a giant picture of the Big No in the entrance hall of my house: BIG NO. There was ink everywhere from that proclamation. The message was: From now onward, it's *NO*.[2] Later on, I executed another calligraphy for the Regent as another special reminder of the Big No, which he has in his office. That No is that you don't give in to things that indulge your reality. There is no special reality beyond reality. That is the Big No, as opposed to the regular no. You *cannot* destroy life. You cannot by any means, for any religious, spiritual, or metaphysical reasons, step on an ant or kill your mosquitoes—at all. That is Buddhism. That is Shambhala. You have to respect *everybody*. You cannot make a random judgment on that at all. That is the rule of the king of Shambhala, and that is the Big No. You can't act on your desires alone. You have to contemplate the details of what needs to be removed and what needs to be cultivated.

On the whole, gentleness is the rule in the Shambhala kingdom. It is actually much more terrifying than kindness, to your surprise. When you are gentle, there's no room for hostility. We like being hostile; we want to be perked up and energized by our negativity. But in Shambhala, we never do that, and we shouldn't do that. However, with Shambhala vision, there is festivity and

his Buddhist lineage of teachings. The Big No is exemplified by the powerful student-teacher encounter that the author describes here, which took place in 1979.

2. Although I wasn't present for the first part of the event, I was invited to the author's house, the Kalapa Court, for the final proclamation of the Big No, which took place about twenty-four hours after the incident began. Chögyam Trungpa, the Dorje Dradul, used an enormous brush to execute a huge calligraphy on a paper banner spread out on the floor of the hallway. When he executed the calligraphy stroke, he crashed the brush down, screaming *NO* at an indescribably deafening volume. Black sumi ink went everywhere. Later, I remember taking my wool skirt to the cleaners, hoping to get the ink out of it—to no avail. The white walls of the hallway had to be repainted.

joyousness, because we are not totally in the dungeon of our neurosis. That cheerfulness is what we call the Great Eastern Sun. The model for the Great Eastern Sun is the sun that shines at ten o'clock in the morning. The sun is no longer the early morning sun, and it is no longer a teenage sun. The sun is about to be full, but it's not quite full. That ten o'clock sun is the Great Eastern Sun.

You may hear what I'm saying and think that it's true. But you have to practice it; you have to do it, sweethearts. We can't just issue messages of philosophy all over the world. We are capable of actually sending up a satellite that would beam down Shambhala or Buddhist slogans twenty-four hours a day. What good would that do? We have to get *ourselves* together.

Please regard yourself as part of the Shambhala kingdom. People say, "Another day, another dollar." But from the Buddhist point of view, we say, "Another breath, another life." We should be proud and very pleased that we can hear these teachings because we have not dropped dead yet! Beyond that, I hope you will have a good time, enjoy your life, and appreciate the information you've received.

A few years ago, His Holiness Karmapa was visiting the United States, and we were working with many different people and organizations to finalize his tour of the country. A Buddhist studies' professor told one of the people working on the arrangements that we should never refer to His Holiness as a king. That is completely missing the point, and it's totally wrong.[3] I am going to write the professor a letter, basically saying exactly that, but I may not put it that politely. We should do things in a humble manner and in a glorious manner, and both of them come together. There's no conflict between the two at all. We need to develop a humble manner, meaning a sense of decorum, without

3. The author's original remark was considerably stronger.

arrogance. But when we invite friends into our home, we shouldn't be shy of showing our guests the silver. Shambhala vision is not based on the creeping humbleness and reasonability of democracy.

143

I hope that we can mingle ourselves together. Please join the Shambhala world. You invite me; I invite you. The world is not all that small. There's a giant world. I appreciate your kindness and goodness. Even after the death of our leader, His Holiness,[4] you have actually made my life longer.

4. His Holiness Rangjung Rigpe Dorje, the Sixteenth Gyalwa Karmapa, the head of the Karma Kagyü lineage of Tibetan Buddhism, passed away from complications of cancer in November 1981. He had visited the United States at the author's invitation three times—in 1974, 1976–77, and 1980. This talk was given in January 1982.

HOW TO KNOW NO

There was a giant No.
That No rained.
That No created a tremendous blizzard.
That No made a dent on the coffee table.
That No was the greatest No of No's in the universe.
That No showered and hailed.
That No created sunshine and simultaneous eclipse of the sun
    and moon.
That No was a lady's legs with nicely heeled shoes.
That No is the best No of all.
When a gentleman smiles, a good man.
That No is the best of the hips.
When you watch the gait of youths as they walk with alternating
    cheek rhythm,
When you watch their behinds,
That No is fantastic thighs, not fat or thin, but taut in their
    strength,
Loveable or leaveable.
That No is shoulders that turn in or expand the chest, sad or
    happy,
Without giving in to a deep sigh.
That No is No of all No's.
Relaxation or restraint is in question.
Nobody knows that Big No,
But we alone know that No.
This No is in the big sky, painted with sumi ink eternally,
This Big No is tattooed on our genitals.
This Big No is not purely freckles or birthmark,

If you know "Not" and have discipline,

Then the ultimate "No" is attained,

Patience will arise along with exertion.

And you are victorious over the maras of the setting sun.

But this Big No is real Big No.
Sky is blue,
Roses are red,
Violets are blue,
And therefore this Big No is No.
Let us celebrate having that monumental No.
The monolithic No stands up and pierces heaven;
Therefore, monolithic No also spreads vast as the ocean.
Let us have great sunshine with this No No.
Let us have full moon with this No No.
Let us have cosmic No.
The cockroaches carry little No No's,
As well as giant elephants in African jungles—
Copulating No No and waltzing No No,
Guinea pig No No,
We find all the information and instructions when a mosquito
    buzzes.
We find some kind of No No.
Let our No No be the greatest motto:
No No for the king;
No No for the prime minister;
No No for the worms of our subjects.
Let us celebrate No No so that Presbyterian preachers can have
    speech impediments in proclaiming No No.
Let our horses neigh No No.
Let the vajra sangha fart No No—
Giant No No that made a great imprint on the coffee table.

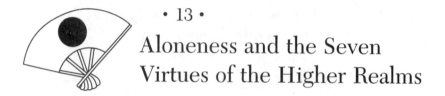

· 13 ·

Aloneness and the Seven Virtues of the Higher Realms

Sadness and aloneness are painful, but at the same time, they are beautiful and real. Out of that comes longing to help others. Being willing to work with others arises spontaneously. Because you care for yourself, therefore, equally you care for others.

FROM THE SHAMBHALA POINT OF VIEW, it is always dawn, and that dawn is the opposite of the setting sun. Our first topic is the dawning of trust, which comes from feeling trustworthy to begin with. When you feel *worthy* of trust, then you can trust. You trust yourself to begin with. Developing trust is also a question of having a sense of humor and not taking things *too* seriously, including yourself. So trust also develops from humbleness. You don't just come to conclusions based on what *you* think. There is respect for the rest of the world, for how things work and how things have evolved. You begin to find that the world around you is quite vivid, real, and obvious. You begin to experience a sense of reality as well as a sense of being, and you develop an uplifted sense of head and shoulders.

Nonetheless, because there is still so much misery, chaos, and degradedness taking place in the world, a certain sadness begins to occur to you. That sadness could be called feeling your heart, actually experiencing your heart fully and thoroughly. Sadness is accompanied by a feeling of aloneness. You wish you could rush to somebody and babble out everything, empty out your heart and share it completely, so that you don't have to feel sad. There's that temptation, but it is not possible. It's like unfulfilled love. When you try to tell somebody how much you love him or her, the other person can't understand why you're making such a dramatic scene. This is the same kind of thing. The feeling of aloneness is an organic development. It is a natural situation. One doesn't actually have to *develop* aloneness. Rather, it is a question of actualizing and realizing aloneness. When that happens, communicating with others becomes very simple.

Sadness is also connected with the absence of cowardice. When you feel brave, free from fear, you also feel sad. That sadness is not the sadness of feeling low and depressed, but it is tearjerking sadness that is always with you. Once you have experienced the bravery that arises from basic goodness, you will also experience sadness and aloneness. In spite of joining in festivities with your relatives, in spite of celebrating the holidays, attending Christmas parties or New Year's parties—whatever you do to try to forget that sadness—sadness will always be there. The more you try to enjoy yourself and the more you *do* enjoy, nonetheless, there is still the constant sadness of being alone.

That sadness also brings tenderness toward oneself. It is quite distinct from depression or the feeling that you want to commit suicide. When people are depressed and lonely—rather than alone—they sometimes want to commit suicide to get rid of their bodies and the environment of depression. With the Shambhala type of sadness, you want to live and help others. Tremendous humor is also present. Nonetheless, there is the sadness of being oneself.

It is as if you were taking a walk in the forest by yourself in the twilight. You hear the birds. You see a glimpse of light coming from the sky: you might see a crescent moon or clusters of stars. The freshness of the greenery with occasional wildflowers is trying to cheer you up. In the distance, dogs are barking. In the distance, a child is crying. Shepherds are calling for their sheep. More likely, in America, in the distance, you hear the roar of the highway, where trucks and cars are making their journeys. Alone in this woodland, you can still hear them and feel them.

You feel a little bit of freshness as the wind begins to blow on your cheeks. You smell the freshness of the woods. You might be startled by an occasional rabbit jumping out of the brush or an occasional bird, startled as you walk by its nest. Pheasants cross your pathway. As twilight goes on, you feel tenderness and sadness for your husband, your wife, your children, your grandparents. You remember the classroom where you studied, learning to spell words when you first went to school. You remember learning to spell your name, learning how to write the letters *j* and *o*, *m* and *a*.

The sadness of being oneself is like taking a walk in the forest, the borderland where things are not completely out of the way. There's still a feeling that this particular woodland is surrounded by other living beings, human beings as well as other beings. You listen to the sound of your footsteps, right, left, right, left. Occasionally you step on a dry twig, which cracks. Maybe there are occasional sounds of flies buzzing. Such sadness and aloneness are painful, but at the same time, they are beautiful and real. Out of that comes longing to help others. Being willing to work with others arises spontaneously. Because you care for yourself, therefore, equally you care for others. That seems to take a certain edge off the sadness. At the same time, sadness still hovers around you.

You begin to see yourself: you realize that you are unique, and you can see how you sometimes make a caricature of yourself. The sadness goes on, constantly. Yet you begin to realize there is something good and constructive about being you as yourself. This experience brings devotion, faith in the great warriors who have made the same journey. It could be devotion toward King Arthur's knights, or any great warriors whose legend inspires you. When caring for others takes place, it brings devotion and dedication to this world in which you grew up. At the same time, caring for others brings renunciation. You are inspired to renounce anything that is without heart: any perversion, selfishness, egotism, and arrogance.

Then, a fundamental wholesomeness arises in oneself, which we call the Great Eastern Sun. It is *Great* because it is vast and inconceivable. One cannot measure how vast the universe is stitch by stitch. Because of that vastness, there is Great *East:* vast possibilities, vast vision, vast aloneness, vast loneliness, vast sadness. One is always in the East, the dawn of wakefulness. One never falls asleep, never gets tired of life or of breathing in and out, as long as we live. One never gets tired of opening one's eyes. One never gets tired of this aloneness, the stirring of the woodland.

The Orient, or the East, is where vision arises. This has nothing to do with a global, geographic, or racial reference point of the East as India, China, Japan, or the rest of Asia. As long as we open our eyes, as long as we breathe out, wherever we are facing, that is East. Wherever you are, you are facing out. You are looking at the East. East is forward, direct, projecting out into this world: Great East.

Then comes the Great Eastern *Sun,* which is quite different from what is traditionally known in Japanese culture as the rising sun. The Great Eastern Sun is the ten o'clock sun, high in the sky, rather than the sun just coming up over the horizon at seven o'clock or eight o'clock. We are talking about a teenage sun. The

151

Great Eastern Sun might be seventeen years old. The Sun is that which shows us the way of discipline, what to do, what not to do. As we cook in the kitchen, the Great Eastern Sun helps us to chop our vegetables, so that we don't cut our fingers. It is quite simple logic: the Great Eastern Sun guides us so that we don't chop off our fingers! The Great Eastern Sun allows us to read the newspaper and find out what's happening in the world. The Great Eastern Sun allows us to greet each other, husband to wife, wife to husband, father to son, father to daughter, children to parents. It allows us to say, "Good morning. How are you this morning?" Even dogs can bark properly in the Great Eastern Sun.

The Great Eastern Sun is simple, straightforward directions about what to do and what not to do. It shows us how to cheer up. When we fly the banner of the Great Eastern Sun, it has a white background, which represents the Great East, and a yellow disk, which represents the Sun. The Great Eastern Sun is a sense of cheerfulness put together with inscrutability and openness, which shows us how to lead our lives.

Out of that rises what is known as the dot in space. Whether you are confused or in a neutral state of mind or your mind is full of subconscious gossip, in any case there is always space. The dot in space is what we call first thought, best thought. In the midst of preoccupations, in the middle of your shower, as you put your pants on, while you dry your hair, while you cook your food, in the midst of all sorts of neutral states of being, the dot is a sharp point that jerks you, shakes you. You are quite easily going through your life, quite naively, and suddenly there's a jerk out of nowhere. First thought, best thought. That experience is the mark of being in the higher realms. Animals, we could say, don't get to see the dot in space. Only human beings have a chance to see the dot in space.

The obstacle to seeing the dot in space is that we're constantly looking for ways to entertain ourselves. When you look up at the sky, if you see a blue sky, you don't quite accept it. You don't want to just look at the blue sky. You want to see *clouds*. We're always looking for something else. Still, the phenomenal world is filled with fantastic possibilities. You don't need to find extra ways to entertain yourself. It is a question of accepting and acknowledging things as they are, learning to accept the ordinariness of extraordinariness. That requires a lot of discipline, particularly in the West. We don't even eat the same meal twice in a week. We are always trying to change one thing into something else, so we resist a daily routine. We try to avoid the familiar. We find it boring.

The Shambhala approach is to befriend what is there, the everyday occurrence, which is real, obvious, and constant. Then first thought, best thought becomes a shocking experience, which shocks us into reality. It may be the same blue sky and the same Volkswagen car that we drive to work every day. But that ordinariness is extraordinary. That is the dichotomy: when you live life in a thoroughly ordinary way, it is extraordinary. I think you have to try it for yourself, and then you'll understand. I can't really explain word by word. I wouldn't even attempt to explain. There is a particular saying in Buddhism that applies at this point: "Even the buddhas' tongues are numb." There are certain things that even the Buddha can't explain. It's a question of doing it. Look at yourself. If you have some sense of open mind at the same time that you are preoccupied, then there might be some kind of jerk that shakes you. That's the closest I can come to explaining. You have to do it.

The next topic is the seven virtues of the higher realms, which distinguish us from the animal realm and which are the ethics of working with the dot in space. These seven virtues, or reminders, will be the cause of seeing the dot in space. Number one is *faith*, or a sense of genuineness. You are not faking anything, and you are not trying to impress anybody. Faith is also appreciation of the Shambhala wisdom. Number two is *discipline.* Your daily life is properly conducted, with no sloppiness. Number three is *daring.* Whenever there is a challenge, you step beyond it. Daring bridges the pond of fear. You're afraid that you might fall in, but with daring, you step over your fear. Number four is *learning,* or studying the Shambhala principles so that you can understand wisdom. Number five is *decorum,* which is cultivating a sense of well-disciplined self-respect. Number six is *modesty.* You don't develop arrogance, but you remain modest and humble. Number seven is *discriminating awareness,* learning to discriminate or distinguish what to do and what not to do.

You have to make an effort to achieve these seven virtues of the higher realms. They are a journey: one virtue leads to the next. So attaining the seven virtues is a linear process, but at the same time, each of them is connected with fundamental discipline. Because of *faith,* one is inspired to have *discipline.* Because of discipline, therefore, one becomes *daring.* Because of daringness, you want to learn more. As you acquire knowledge from *learning,* you develop *decorum.* Because of your decorum and elegance, you begin to develop *modesty* and humbleness. You are not bloated. And because of your humbleness, you begin to have *discriminating awareness,* knowing how to distinguish one thing from another, what to accept and what to reject.

By practicing the virtues of the higher realms, you develop the capability to bring about *the* first thought. Sometimes your so-called first thought is filled with aggression, resentment, or some other habitual pattern. At that point, you're experiencing second thought rather than the real first thought. It's not fresh. It is like wearing a shirt for the second time. It's been worn before, so you can't quite call it a clean shirt. That is like missing the first thought. First thought is fresh thought. By practicing the virtues of the higher realms, you can bring about the fresh first thought.

It is possible. Then you begin to see the dot in space much more clearly and precisely. Of course, these seven disciplines are not conducted with a long face, but with the joy of taking a walk in the woods, with a sense of rejuvenating and refreshing oneself.

In Tibet, when children reach the age of seven or eight, we let them use knives. Sometimes they cut themselves, but most of the time they don't, because they are old enough to learn to use a knife properly. They learn to be cautious, and they learn that they are actually capable. At the age of eight, children in a Tibetan farming village may be put in charge of a herd of animals, including the young lambs and calves. We send the children out in the mountains to take care of their animals. They have to pay heed and bring the sheep and cows back to the village when it is milking time. They have to be sure the little ones are safe, and they are told ways to ward off wild animals. All that knowledge is passed on to the children.

So children in Tibet don't play all the time. They play, but they work at the same time. In that way, they develop a sense of how to lead life and how to grow up. I think one of the problems in the West is that children have too much access to toys and not enough access to reality. They can't actually go out and do anything constructive by themselves. They have to imagine that they're working. It's healthy to introduce young people to the real world, instead of just saying, "He's a child. He can't do that. We are the adults. We have to take care of the children." The limitations we place on children are quite hypothetical. We have so many preconceptions about young people. Children can take care of young animals, just as they learn to read and write. They do it very well.

In my country, there were very few schools. Children were mostly taught by their parents and grandparents. They didn't regard learning to read and write as a duty. Children today often say, "Do we *have* to go to school?" But in Tibet, they regarded it as a natural part of their growing process, as much as herding cattle or sheep. There was less preconception and more realism in children's upbringing. There was much more of a sense of becoming an individual, being less dependent on others. So in that way, learning to be alone in one's early years can be the beginning of warrior training.

We've been here on this earth for millions of years. Confusion has been handed down to us, and we are busy making confusion for others—by trying to make money from others or by coming up with all sorts of gimmicks, all sorts of easy ways to deal with things. In the mechanical age, there is too much reference to comfort. For parents today, sending their children to school is viewed as relief. You park the children in school for part of the day, and then you have time for yourself. A lot of problems come from that kind of laziness. We don't really want to deal with problems; we don't want to dirty our hands anymore. Reality has been handed down to you through somebody else's experiences, and you don't want to experience reality for yourself. Bad information and laziness have been handed down to us, and we become the product of that mentality.

Then nobody wants to take a walk in the woods, certainly not by themselves. If you do go for a walk, you bring at least three or four people with you and your camping gear. You bring along butane gas, so that you don't have to collect wood to make a fire in the woods. You cook your food on your butane stove, and you certainly don't sleep on the ground. You have a comfortable pad in your little tent. Everything is shielded from reality. I'm not particularly suggesting that we become naturalists and forget about modern technology. But one has to be alone. One has to really learn to face aloneness. When you get a little prick from brushing your hand against a branch in the woods, you don't immediately have to put a Band-Aid on it. You can let yourself bleed a little bit. You may not even need a Band-Aid. The scratch might heal by itself.

Things have become so organized and institutionalized. Technology is excellent. It is the product of centuries and centuries of work. Hundreds of thousands of people worked to achieve the technology we enjoy. It's great. It's praiseworthy. But at the same time, the way we use technology is problematic. Ça va?

One needs discipline with enjoyment. In the Shambhala tradition, the sitting practice of meditation is the fundamental discipline. At the beginning, there is resistance to sitting on a meditation cushion and being still. Once you pass that resistance, that barrier, that particular Great Wall of China, then you are inside the Great Wall, and you can appreciate the uprightness, purity, and freshness.

If there is a temptation to stop paying attention, you bring yourself back. It's like herding a group of cows who would like to cross the fence into the neighbor's field. You have to push them back, but you do it with a certain sense of enjoyment. Discipline is a very personal experience, extremely personal. It's like hugging somebody. When you give somebody a hug, you wonder, "Who is going to stop hugging first? Shall I do it? Or will the other person?"

You have such enthusiasm and basic goodness. Although you may not believe it, it is dazzling in you. We can communicate the vision of the Great Eastern Sun to others, for the very fact that we and they both have it within ourselves. Suppose everybody believed that they had only one eye. We would have to let everybody know that they have two eyes. In the beginning, there would be a lot of people against us, saying that it's not true. They would accuse us of giving out the wrong information, because they'd been told and they believed that they only have one eye. Eventually, however, somebody would realize that they actually had two eyes, and then that knowledge would begin to spread. The Shambhala wisdom is actually as stupid or literal as that. It's very obvious. But because of our habitual tendencies and other obstacles, we've never allowed ourselves to believe in it or look at it at all. Once we begin to do so, we will realize that it's possible and true.

THE MEEK
Powerfully Nonchalant and Dangerously Self-Satisfying

In the midst of thick jungle
Monkeys swing,
Snakes coil,
Days and nights go by.
Suddenly I witness you,
Striped like sun and shade put together.
You slowly scan and sniff, perking your ears,
Listening to the creeping and rustling sounds:
You have supersensitive antennae.
Walking gently, roaming thoroughly,
Pressing paws with claws,
Moving with the sun's camouflage,
Your well-groomed exquisite coat has never been touched
     or hampered by others.
Each hair bristles with a life of its own.
In spite of your feline bounciness and creeping slippery
     accomplishment,
Pretending to be meek,
You drool as you lick your mouth.
You are hungry for prey—
You pounce like a young couple having orgasm;
You teach zebras why they are black and white;
You surprise haughty deer, instructing them to have a sense
     of humor along with their fear.
When you are satisfied roaming in the jungle,
You pounce as the agent of the sun:
Catching pouncing clawing biting sniffing—

Such meek tiger achieves his purpose.
Glory be to the meek tiger!
Roaming, roaming endlessly,
Pounce, pounce in the artful meek way,
Licking whiskers with satisfying burp.
Oh, how good to be tiger!

· 14 ·

The King of the Four Seasons

A kingdom isn't always a country. The kingdom is your household, and your household is a kingdom. In a family, you may have a father, a mother, sisters, brothers. That setup is in itself a small kingdom for you to practice and work with as its king or queen. Those who don't have a family can work on how they schedule and conduct their own personal discipline properly and thoroughly.

IT IS NECESSARY TO UNDERSTAND the concept of the Great Eastern Sun in contrast to the setting sun. The setting sun is not abstract; it is something real that you can overcome. The setting-sun world is not Americana, nor are we saying that the medieval world is the world of the Great Eastern Sun. Rather, we are talking about overcoming frivolity and becoming a decent person.

The dot in space—first thought, best thought—automatically overcomes the setting sun. Just the thought of the setting sun is second thought, although it may sometimes be disguised as first thought. But it is not the best thought, at all. You have to give up all those second thoughts, third thoughts, and other thoughts up to even the eighth or ninth level. When you begin to give up, then you go back to first thought. When you almost despair and lose heart, that provides a sense of open space, where things begin anew.

The loneliness of the setting-sun world is very intense. Often people commit suicide because of it. Those who survive in the setting sun without committing suicide must maintain their "trips," pretending that they are making a fabulous journey. I visited Esalen Institute some time ago. Everybody there was having a *groovy* time, as they would say there, trying to avoid reality. The whole setup is based on the avoidance of reality; therefore, you have a *groovy* time. It's such a *groovy* place, such a fabulous place. You don't ever have to do any work there. They would never ask you to use a shovel to dig up the earth and plant flowers in the garden. The flowers are there already for you to pick or wear in your hair. Such a *groovy* place with all sorts of schools of thought, schools of massage, and physical trainings of all kinds provided to make you younger—so that you can forget impermanence.

It is a place to be a teenager, even if you are ninety years old. Some of the older people actually behave like teenagers. In fact, they talk like them and think like them. The setting-sun philosophy is extremely appealing to some people, because it goes along with their own deception. To them, deception is referred to as *potential.* When people say that so and so has great potential, often they mean that so and so has very thick, dense deception. The dot in space cuts through hypocrisy of that kind and brings about the decorum that is based on truth and natural dignity. When you sneeze, you don't have to apologize to anybody, just because you happen to have a body and you sneeze. Decorum is natural dignity and natural elegance that don't have to be cultivated by means of deception. You don't have to go to Esalen Institute to find it.

Togetherness is another word for decorum. Such wonderful decorum is a sense of naturally fitting into the situation. You don't have to tailor your outfit. It fits naturally, with dignity and beauty. That decorum, or genuineness, is the result of seeing the dot in space. From that, we begin to develop fearlessness, or nonfear. First, you see fear. Then, fear is overcome through the sense of decorum, and finally, fearlessness is achieved by means of seeing the dot in space.

Fearlessness is like a tiger, roaming in the jungle. It is a tiger who walks slowly, slimly, in a self-contained way. At the same time, the tiger is ready to jump—not out of paranoia but because of natural reflex, because of a smile and sense of humor. Shambhala people are not regarded as self-serious people. They see humor everywhere, in all directions, and they find beauty everywhere as well. Humor, in this sense, is not mocking others, but it is appreciating natural funniness.

When you achieve such fearlessness, then you can abandon your giant backpack, where you carry all sorts of things to protect yourself from nature. You begin to realize that nature has its own quality, and you begin to live with nature. In the midst of fearlessness, a sense of ease arises. Because of the ease and naturalness of fearlessness, you feel that you are not being attacked, so you don't have to defend yourself. There is no paranoia. With that ease and looseness, your head and shoulders begin to perk up. Ordinarily, our image of head and shoulders is a tight posture. But when this tremendous ease takes place, you feel that you are just there, like the sunshine, so brilliant, so natural. So the posture of head and shoulders is quite natural. It is simply viewing the universe without hassle.

Out of that arises natural hierarchy. Hierarchy, according to the dictionary, is a pyramidal power structure that you climb until you get to the top. But we are talking about natural hierarchy, which takes place when for the first time somebody experiences the Great Eastern Sun and sees its humor.

It is like the four seasons. Cold winter turns into inviting spring, which brings luscious summer, which gives us the productive autumn, which then goes back to winter. The discipline of winter gives way again to the beautiful unfolding process of spring. The spring melts the snow, bringing the exposed earth of summer. Then again, the possibilities of summer cannot last throughout the whole year. So the discipline of autumn occurs. As autumn comes to an end, we develop the one-pointedness, the one-mindedness, of winter. We can go on, again and again. The one-pointedness of winter begins to lose its grip, its grasp, and it turns into spring. Flowers begin to develop, and the trees are softened by their potential blossoms. Spring is willing to become extravagant summer; then the extravaganza of summer occurs. Nonetheless, there is some comptroller or administrator who says, "Enough is enough."

Then summer turns into autumn, which brings us back to the practicality of the winter. We enjoy the fires burning in our homes. True reality occurs in the winter. Human beings are different from animals. Human beings have to wear layer upon layer of clothes to face the winter: undershirt, T-shirt, warm top shirt, sweater, jacket, topcoat. All those layers almost recreate the abundance of autumn, but when we're finally fortified enough to face the winter, it is too late, and spring comes. The gaiety of the spring brings possibilities that truth may be true, although watching the vulnerable buds in the trees, one never knows. There could be a sudden snowstorm or a sudden frost. Spring is like a person about to smile, who hasn't shown their teeth but is just grinning. Then we show our teeth and we smile properly in the summer. That brings the autumn again. Then, reality is reality. Enough is enough! In winter, we bake good bread, eat our gruel, and enjoy the grain from the harvest that we achieved in the autumn. We could go on . . .

By the way, ladies and gentlemen, that is natural hierarchy.

A king or queen exists. That king appreciates being king, which is like the spring. The spring king is crowned or enthroned by the subjects. So the king does not become arrogant or take pride in himself alone. The king appreciates that the subjects have made him their king. The king appreciates the whole process, which is the king-*dom*. Let the kingdom flourish, let us have freedom, and let every subject enjoy the kingdom. Let our children have good schools, let the workers have good working environments, and let the factories produce their best abundance of food and clothing. Let all the subjects be so elegant and beautiful. That is summer.

Then there is the autumn aspect of the kingdom: let us not indulge, but let us have some system of government. Let us have a good constitution. Let us have a real sense of working properly with each other. That brings us to the winter. When the kingdom is cold and troublesome, we don't regard it as an attack or as depression in the kingdom. We regard it as an opportunity to show how brave and arrogant we can be as subjects of this kingdom. In that way, natural hierarchy is based on the four seasons.

A kingdom isn't always a country. The kingdom is your household, and your household is a kingdom. In a family, you may have a father, a mother, sisters, brothers. That setup is in itself a small kingdom for you to practice and work with as its king or queen. Those who don't have a family can work on how they schedule and conduct their own personal discipline properly and thoroughly. You eat breakfast, lunch, and dinner. You meet your friends, do your work, do your studies. There is automatically a pattern involved. That pattern should be a joyous one, a happy one, rather than merely obligatory.

I see and hear from a lot of people for whom the regularity of life is a pain. They wish they had a different menu every minute. You have to settle down, somewhere. You have to work on having a regular life, a disciplined life. Traditionally, Shambhalians stay in a job for at least five years. In my case, it has been forty years, and I haven't had the faintest temptation to change my job. The more discipline that occurs, the more joyous it becomes. That is a very important point in the Shambhala training.

You can help others to overcome frivolity. Based on your own inspiration, you can help people get out of situations that they're stuck in. Usually, frivolity occurs when people are stuck, literally, in one place. They go to the same place and listen to the same music, do the same things, eat the same food. You can help create a change of attitude, a change of environment for them. With your own Shambhala inspiration, you can bring others into a different environment. At the beginning, they might find it slightly awkward; nonetheless, they will probably find it more enjoyable.

Acting as a leader for others has to be based on your own development, how confident you feel in yourself, and how much training you have. If you feel capable and trained and processed enough in your daily life, then you can launch into working with others. It is a question of your own personal development. From the Buddhist point of view, friends who create discipline and lighten up our ego are called the *sangha*. In the Shambhala culture, we call such friends *warriors*. Warriors can cheer one another up and together create a warrior society. *Warrior,* by the way, is a term that applies to both men and women.

There is a powerful bond between yourselves and myself. We share the Great Eastern Sun together, which is very powerful and important, whether in times of trouble or no trouble. Together, we share in caring for this world, which means that we share the Shambhala Kingdom together. We share the Shambhala tradition. We are brothers and sisters, or father and child in the Great Eastern Sun.

Welcome to the Shambhala world. I'm so pleased that you are here to liberate yourselves from personal burden and to take on other people's burden with compassion. Don't be lazy. The world needs you, very badly, so try to apply these teachings to your day-to-day life situation. Please don't forget. We have a lot of work to do. Hundreds of thousands of people need tremendous help.

I think almost everything has been said. There's nothing left unsaid, except one last thing, which is the parting of friendship. I would like to make a toast to the best of the students, the best of the listeners, and to the great would-be warriors of the future. No doubt about it. To the warriors of the past, present, and future, I would like to raise a toast: To fearlessness!

SEASONING LIFE

Children run barefooted
Old men with walking sticks sniff fresh air
Spring is good—we all blossom

Active time for the umbrellas
Muddy path for the horses
Chrysanthemums and peonies are gorgeous
Summer is imperial festival

A drop from heaven on my head
I discover it is merely apple
Prosperous time
We are attacked by hailstorms of grain

Home is precious
White world is cold
However, the icicle tunes are melodic
The emperor is returning to his palace

PART FOUR

POWERFUL

The remaining chapters in the book are written as though you were there. You're invited to participate. Please come along and join the audience. The speaker has arrived, so take your seat. The talk is about to begin . . .

· 15 ·

The Basic Gasp of Goodness

GOOD MORNING. I'm so pleased to be here. I am struck by your sweetness and your kindness. I hope there may be some underlying cynicism as well. We open by saying "Good morning" because the Great Eastern Sun never sets. We don't have much time to discuss the great depth of possibilities of Shambhala vision, but we will do our best.

We are going back to basic goodness. Why do we possess basic goodness at all? Why is it basic? Why is it good, for heaven's sake? Basic goodness is based on your first mind, first thought. Before thought, you have a gasp, a sharp in-breath, *Ah-ah!*[1] Whatever you think, even before you think, before you gasp, there is space. There is purity. There is *Ah-ah!* Sometimes you feel so dumb that you can't think of anything. Sometimes you think you're so intelligent, and you can't think of anything. There is just *Ah-ah!*

That is basic goodness. It is not good as opposed to bad. It is basic vacantness, just vacant, pure. That basic gasp, basic awake,

---

1. If you breathe in sharply through your mouth, so that you can hear your breath, you will be approximating the sound made here by the author.

basic *Ah-ah!*—just before you hiccup—is basic Shambhala mind altogether. Out of that, believe it or not, fearlessness arises. Fear is another kind of *Ah-ah! Fearlessness* is also *Ah-ah!* Once you realize that basic gasp, you are fearless.

Out of that, you begin to realize individual dignity, and you settle down as you are, as basic being, as Joe Schmidt, Mary Newton, Tom Smith. Isn't it wonderful to be Tom Smith? Isn't it fantastic to be Mary Newton? Please smile. You have a self-snug grin in you, where not only your mouth laughs but your heart also laughs. That sense of joy and greatness is always there.

By the way, this is not a theory. I, Lord Mukpo, have experienced it myself. You might refer to me or address me as Lord Mukpo. Lord Mukpo is both my title and my name. Lord is like the sky. Mukpo is like the sunshine in the midst of the sky. I grew up as a lord of Tibet. Mukpo is my family name, my true name, my real name. Literally, it means "dark." Mukpo is like the darkness after the sun sets, but with an interesting twist. When the physical sun sets, Mukpo shines. Mukpo sunshine. Mukpo—that is my name. That is my clan.

Ladies and gentlemen, I wanted to introduce myself properly to you as Lord Mukpo because all of you are part of my clan. Even in the darkest of the dark age, there is always light. That light comes with a smile, the smile of Shambhala, the smile of fearlessness, the smile of realizing the best of the best of human potential.

We have much more to discuss. But for now, I would like you not to speculate but just to be. Look at your mind. Just be. Hold your posture, be upright, hold up your head and shoulders. Sit cross-legged in good warrior posture. This is not a gloomy situation. We are at the height of the best and most cheerful world that has ever been known—which is called enlightened society.

Let us smile. Hold up your posture. When I count three, click in. One, two, ready . . . We are the happiest people in the entire world. We are the most enlightened society in the entire world. It's very moving. It's very real. We are not kidding ourselves.

I would like to explain the warrior's bow to you. This bow is done from a standing or sitting position. You may be sitting in a chair, kneeling, or sitting cross-legged in the posture of meditation. You bow as a sign of greeting. You bow as a sign of respect. When you start a meeting, you may bow, and you bow at the end as well.

When you bow, your posture is upright. Your torso, your shoulders, and your neck are all held upright. You sit up like a good arrow. Then your arms make the bōw.[2] You place your hands on your thighs, with your arms held out a little from your torso, rounded into a gentle bōw shape. Then, when you bow, it is like shooting directly at a target. The bōw and arrow bow together.

Why don't we try it? Can you do it? Sit up straight like an arrow, and then make your hands, arms, and shoulders into the bōw. Now you are ready to bow. When you bow, don't look for danger. Don't look for obstacles. Just bow completely.

Let's practice it again. Be up, up. Include your shoulders. Your head and shoulders are upright. Then, keeping your head straight, bend forward, bring your shoulders along, and bend down. Bend down more. Then let your neck go over your shoulders a little bit. Finally, bend from your neck.

Exchanging a bow is like sharing a kiss with your lover. First, you turn your face toward your lover. Then, you bend your neck toward your lover, and your lover bends their neck toward you as well. Then you embrace together. That is the example of how to surrender with a bow.

I appreciate your presence here, and I love you all. Thank you very much.

2. The author is speaking here about bowing, as surrendering or bending down, and he is also talking about a bōw and arrow. To distinguish the bow from the bōw, I have included the diacritical mark ō, to make the long *o* in "bōw and arrow."

· 16 ·

Helping Others

THE PURPOSE OF THE SHAMBHALA TRAINING is to help others, to save others, and to cure others' pain. That is the key point. There are so many confused people and psychotics in the world, and it is your duty, *our* duty, to help them. How you do that depends on what profession you are engaged in. You may be involved with child care. You may be involved with the fine arts or with making movies. You may be involved with gardening and raising plants in a nursery. The point is to help others through any means you can, through your particular profession, whatever it may be.

In order to help somebody, first raise your head and shoulders. Then, don't try to convert people to your dogma, but just encourage them. Whatever profession they have—whether they are dairy farmers, lawyers, or cab drivers—first, raise *your* consciousness, and then talk to them on their own terms. Don't try to make them join the Shambhala club or the Buddhist scene or anything like that. Just let them *be* in their own way. Have a drink, have dinner, make a date with them—just keep it simple.

The main point is definitely not to get them to join your organization. That is the *least* of the points. The main point is to help others be good human beings *in their own way*. We are not into converting people. They may convert themselves, but we just keep in touch with them. Usually, in any organization, people cannot keep themselves from drawing others into their scene or their trip, so to speak. That is not our plan. Our plan is to make sure that individuals, whoever we meet, have a good life. At the same time, you should keep in contact with people, in whatever way you can. That's very important, not because we're into converting others, but because we are into communicating.

When you are trying to help others, you will probably feel lonely, feeling that you don't have a partner to work with. You may also begin to feel that the world is so disordered. I personally feel sadness, always. You feel sad, but you don't really want to burst into tears. You feel embryonic sadness. There are hundreds of thousands of people who need your help, which makes you feel sad, so sad. It's not that you need someone to keep you company, but it is sad because you feel the sense of aloneness, and others do not. Many people have this experience. For example, I have a friend and student named Baird Bryant whom I've worked with for many years. He is a filmmaker, and we worked together on several films. I can see that he has that kind of sadness. He wishes that something could be done for others, that something could be made right. He has that sadness, aloneness, and loneliness, which I appreciate very much. In fact, I have learned from witnessing my friend's experience.

There are two types of sadness. The first is when you look at a beautiful flower and you wish you could *be* that flower. It is so beautiful. The second is that nobody else understands that flower. It's so beautiful, utterly beautiful, so magnificent. Nobody understands that. In spite of that beauty, people are killing each other. They're destroying each other. They go to the bar and get drunk instead of thinking of that beautiful flower.

175

That sadness is a key point, ladies and gentlemen. In the back of your head, you hear a beautiful flute playing, because you are so sad. At the same time, the melody cheers you up. You are not on the bottom of the barrel of the world or in the Black Hole of Calcutta. In spite of being sad and devastated, there is something lovely taking place. There is some smile, some beauty. In the Shambhala world, we call that *daringness*. In the Buddhist language, we call it compassion. Daringness is sympathetic to oneself. There is no suicidal sadness involved *at all*. Rather, there is a sense of big, open mind in dealing with others, which is beautiful, wonderful.

We find ourselves shedding tears at the same time that we are smiling. We are crying and laughing at once. That is the ideal Shambhalian mentality: we cry and we smile at the same time. Isn't it wonderful? A flower needs sunshine together with raindrops to blossom so beautifully. For that matter, a rainbow is made out of the tears falling from our eyes, mixed with a shot of sunshine. That is how a rainbow becomes a rainbow—sunshine mixed with tears. From that point of view, the Shambhala philosophy is the philosophy of a rainbow.

Daringness also means that you are not afraid to let go when you help others. You wouldn't hesitate to say to someone, "Don't you think you should be more daring, Mr. Joe Schmidt? I see that you're at the end of your rope. You're not doing so good. Don't you think you should pick up your end of the rope and smile with me?" A Shambhala person can help others in that way—in many ways. A Shambhala person can also *demonstrate* warriorship to others. If I slump down like this, what does this posture say? Can somebody please answer? Please talk into the microphone so that we get this on tape. People of future generations have to hear what you're saying. We are making history, you see.

STUDENT: That posture looks sleepy and floppy. It doesn't communicate much of anything.

DORJE DRADUL OF MUKPO: Yes. OK. Now, how about when I sit up like this?

SECOND STUDENT: There's a sense of joy that just spills over.

DORJE DRADUL OF MUKPO: Well . . . we have to be careful about saying "joy." We're not only cultivating joy. This posture is also cultivating strength and the ability to work with others. You don't just purely feel good, right? Thank you very much. Could someone else say something? The young lady over there?

THIRD STUDENT: The second, upright, posture is certainly more warriorlike than the slumped-down one. Confidence and strength are qualities that also occur to me.

DORJE DRADUL OF MUKPO: How would you explain a Shambhala warrior to somebody who just came out of McDonald's?

STUDENT: I would try to communicate to them that the Shambhala warrior does not go out to fight like the warriors I learned about in history class. I would try to communicate that the Shambhala warrior is fearless, ready to meet the world head-on, not necessarily charging into it, but being open to anything that comes in. The Shambhala warrior is fearless and brave.

DORJE DRADUL OF MUKPO: Jolly good. That's wonderful. Thank you, sweetheart. You make me melt. Young warrior, your goodness makes me melt. Thank you very much.

In communicating with others, we can definitely make a profound statement. We can communicate with others about their state of being, their own pain, their own pleasure. We don't feel that this world is bad. We feel that this world has basic goodness. We can communicate that.

We don't have to run away from this world. We don't have to feel harsh and *deprived.* We can contribute a lot to the world, and

177

we can RAISE ourselves up in this world. We should feel *so good*. This world is the best world. As we raise up the world, we should also feel good, both at once, right? There are all sorts of ways to do that. If you drive into the mountains with a friend, you may see the mountain deer. They're so well groomed, although they don't live on a farm. They have tremendous head and shoulders, and their horns are so beautiful. The birds who land on your porch are also well groomed, because they are not conditioned by ordinary conditionality. They are themselves. They are so good.

Look at the sun. The sun is shining. Nobody polishes the sun. The sun just shines. Look at the moon, the sky, the world at its best. Unfortunately, we human beings try to fit everything into conditionality. We try to make something out of nothing. We have messed everything up. That's *our* problem. We have to go back to the sun and the moon, to dragons, tigers, lions, garudas.[1] We can

1. A mythical bird.

be like the blue sky, sweethearts, and the clouds so clean, so beautiful.

We don't have to try *too* hard to find ourselves. We haven't really lost anything; we just have to tune in. The majesty of the world is always there, always there, even from the simplest point of view. In order to help others, we aren't going to conquer anybody and turn them into a serf, although sometimes we might have to conquer their confusion. Human beings need education so badly, in order to raise themselves to a higher level of existence.

So there's one last thing, which is said very ironically. Am I mad? Or are you mad? As far as I can see, I'm not mad. I appreciate this beautiful world so much, which might mean that I am mad. You could put me in the nuthouse. *Or* we could all go into the nuthouse. I'm only joking!

In order to help others, stay with the sadness. Stay with the sadness completely. Sadness is your first perception of somebody. Then you might feel anger, as the methodology to help them. You

179

might have to say rather angrily to somebody, "Now, pull yourself together, OK?" We can't just view the world as if nothing bad had ever happened. That won't do. We have to get into the world. We have to involve ourselves in the setting sun. When you first see a person, you see that person with Great Eastern Sun possibilities. When you actually work with that person, you have to help him or her overcome the setting sun, making sure that the person is no longer involved with setting-sun possibilities.

To do that, you have to have humor, self-existing humor, and you have to hold the moth in your hand, but not let it go into the flame. That's what helping others means. Ladies and gentlemen, we have so much responsibility. A long time ago, people helped one another in this way. Now people just talk, talk, and talk. They read books, they listen to music, but they never actually help anyone. They never use their bare hands to save a person from going crazy. We have that responsibility. Somebody has to do it. It turns out to be us. We've *got* to do it, and we can do it with a smile, not with a long face.

STUDENT: Why do you think *we've* got to do it?

DORJE DRADUL OF MUKPO: Why do *we* have to do it? Somebody has to do it. Suppose you're very badly hurt in a car crash. Why does anybody have to help you? Somebody's got to do it. In this case, we have that responsibility, that absolute responsibility. As far as I'm concerned, I'm willing to take responsibility, and I appreciate the opportunity very much. I've been a prince, I've been a monk, I've been a householder: I've experienced all kinds of human life. And I appreciate life. I do not resent being born on this earth *at all.* I appreciate it. I love it. That's why I am called *Lord* Mukpo: because I love this world so much.

The world doesn't put me off *at all.* Due to my education and my studies with my teacher, I love the world. I love to go to New York City, for instance, because I love the chaos. Sometimes I wonder whether I'm a maniac, because I just want to *save everybody.* Perhaps I am. But then the *dralas*[2] tell me, "No, you are not a maniac." The death of His Holiness Karmapa has left me with a lot of responsibility, but I'm quite happy to take it on.

SECOND STUDENT: I'm very glad to meet you finally. But it's a little disconcerting to come here out of self-interest and to find out that I'm about to go out and help everybody else.

DORJE DRADUL OF MUKPO: You have to help yourself first, so you'll be ready to help others. Tomorrow there will be a transmission of how to do it, how to actually *be* a warrior. In connection with that, I would like everybody to think about how to help others. Last night, I couldn't help myself. I had to present the initial realization and understanding of how you can actually *be,* to begin with. Tonight has been more pragmatic, more of the working situation. Tomorrow we can go beyond that.

I'm *so proud* of you, absolutely so proud. You've all had many samsaric experiences in the past, but at this point, I'm so proud of you. I would very very much like to thank you. Very much. On the whole, I would really *very VERY* much like to say, ladies and gentlemen, that you are all worthy subjects of the Shambhala kingdom. We are one. In order to create enlightened society, men and women like you are very necessary. Thank you very much.

Tonight, I would like to introduce the Shambhala warrior's cry. Chanting this cry is a way to rouse your head and shoulders, a way to rouse a sense of uplifted dignity. It is also a way to invoke the power of windhorse and the energy of basic goodness. We might call it a battle cry, as long as you understand that this particular battle is fighting against aggression, conquering aggression, rather than promoting hatred or warfare. We could say that the warrior's cry celebrates victory over war, victory over aggression.

2. In the Shambhala teachings, the manifestation, strength, or bravery that transcends or conquers aggression. Sometimes translated as "war gods," *dralas* means "being above or beyond war."

It is also a celebration of overcoming obstacles. The warrior's cry goes like this: Ki Ki So So. *Ki* is primordial energy, similar to the idea of *chi* in the Chinese martial arts, as in T'ai Chi Ch'uan. *So* is furthering or extending that energy of ki and extending the power of Ki Ki So So altogether. Let us close our meeting by shouting "Ki Ki So So" three times.[3] Sitting in good warrior posture, with your hands on your hips, hold your head and shoulders and shout:

Ki Ki So So

Ki Ki So So

Ki Ki So So

Good morning.

3. *Ki Ki So So* is a traditional victory chant in Tibet. It is often chanted during a ritual purification ceremony called a *lhasang*, which involves the burning of juniper and passing sacred objects through the smoke. It is also chanted when one reaches the top of a mountain pass. The traveler places a flag in a rock cairn on top of the pass and chants the warrior's cry. Chögyam Trungpa describes how he performed this ritual during his escape from Tibet: "Ahead of us lay the very high pass of Sharkong La; it was extremely steep and the weather was very stormy, so when we had got about half way up we camped for the night. . . . The next morning we returned to the climb. . . . When we reached the top of the pass, I, Kino Tulku and Akong Tulku dismounted to give the traditional traveller's shout of victory, after which we duly added a flag to the cairn" (*Born in Tibet*, p. 176).

SANITY IS JOYFUL

Riding on a white horse,
Carrying the full blade sword,
Holding the victorious view—without wearing glasses—
As I hear the fluttering of the banner of victory,
As I smell horse dung,
As I hear the troops chattering along with their suits of armor—
I feel so romantic
And so brave.
As I carry the bow and arrow in my hand—
It is better than making love to a maiden:
As I defeat the enemy, I feel so good,
I feel so compassionate—
Love and kindness to my enemies.
That is why I will say,
Ki Ki So So!
Maybe the Dorje Dradul is mad,
But on the other hand
The sanest person on earth is the Dorje Dradul.
Ki Ki So So!

D. D. M.

Transmission

GOOD MORNING, EVERYONE. Tonight is your final confirmation as Shambhala warriors. Ironically, the warriors of Shambhala do not create war. The word *warrior,* by itself, may mean a creator of war or a warmonger, but the warriors of Shambhala are the opposite—of course. The Shambhala warrior does not create war, *at all,* but is somebody who creates peace. The warriors of Shambhala are those who are interested in subjugating their own desires for war and for aggression. Last night we talked about sadness. That quality is precisely the heart of warriorship. The warrior is completely in tune with people and with their various levels of emotionality. We are the opposite of warmongers.

How beautiful is red! How beautiful is yellow! How beautiful is green! How beautiful is blue! How beautiful is gray! When we look around, how beautiful it is. How beautiful to see a person sitting upright enjoying their meal. How good to see a person taking a shower, lathering their hair. How good it is, a person shaving. How good it is, the ladies combing their hair. They comb their hair as if it were the mane of a Shambhala tiger or a lion's mane—whether they use hair dryers or not.

We are always good warriors of Shambhala: good tigers, good lions, good garudas, good dragons, with great teeth, beautiful shiny faces, beautiful hands. How beautiful the demeanor of human existence. The Shambhala world is an individual world. At the same time, it is a world that we share. When we relate with the rest of the world, we should be well groomed. That is one of the very first principles of Shambhala decorum.

I would like to discuss the concept of a Shambhala lord a bit further. *Lord* is an Old English word. In French, lord is *seigneur*, and in Spanish, it is *señor*. *Lord* here does not mean "overlord." An overlord uses other people, regarding them as serfs, as people with no dignity. An overlord uses others as dishwashers and bus-boys or as rickshaw haulers. In this case, when we talk about a lord, when we talk about Lord Mukpo, we are talking about iden-tifying ourselves with the sun and the moon.

Lord Mukpo is not going to kill people or make people work in the sewerage system or in the lowest of the lowest of the lowest places that you can think of. Lord Mukpo is brilliance. As lords and ladies of Shambhala, we can be together with the sun and the moon, the moon of skillful means and the sun of brilliance, which are the masculine and the feminine principles. The lords and la-dies of Shambhala dare not take advantage of their own inade-quacy or the inadequacy of others.

Lord or *lady* here also means power, a sense of reality in which real strength can be wielded by every one of us. Power is not power over somebody else, in the sense of an overlord. In this case, power is the power to be yourself. The original lord inspires that power in you. You have power to open your bloody[1] eyes, your bloody nose, your bloody mouth. You have bloody power, wonderful power, extraordinary power.

---

1. The word *bloody* here is used to intensify or lend force to the word it precedes. This usage, according to the *Oxford English Dictionary*, goes back to the end of the

On the whole, the warriors of Shambhala are not afraid of anybody. We hold ourselves with good head and shoulders. With good head and shoulders, we do not subjugate ourselves or submit to anybody else—bloody anybody else. We can be *ourselves*, my lords and ladies.

Let us hold up our head and shoulders, OK? This will be the transmission of the power of warriorship. Hold up your spine. Open your eyes. Head and shoulders at its best. I want you to say the cry of the Shambhala warriors after me. When you say that, you receive the transmission, and you will have the power altogether.

OK. First, hold yourselves up. OK? Ready? Repeat after me: *Ki Ki So So.*

Ki Ki So So

Let us bow. Let us be humble and bow much more. Make a good bow, a gentle bow. Power and strength have occurred already. You don't have to hang on to that. Now you can surrender; you can really bow.

PLEASE smile. Have fun! It is as if the span of an eagle's wings were suddenly given to you. As if the haughtiness and the head and shoulders of the deer were given to you. As if the quickness of the fish were given to you. I am overjoyed to share this with you. I have been holding back for so long!

There is a mutual understanding between all of you and myself, my heritage, my lineage. With your concern for humanity, we will surely help others. That seems to be the case, and that seems to be the point. That seems to be the reason why we are here together: to help others.

---

seventeenth century, when aristocratic rowdies were called "bloods." The phrase "bloody drunk," for example, meant as drunk as a blood, or as drunk as a lord.

BATTLE CRY

Riding on the horse who is impeccably, militarily trained,
Carrying the six weapons with one's head and shoulders up for
the warfare.
Contemplating whether you are fighting in the name of passion
or aggression—
Should you crush a jar of honey with your fist or slash it with a
sword?—
I am wondering whether I am what I am.
My deeds and thoughts will synchronize in the name of great
dralas.
I wonder whether I may kiss the sword
Or lick the blade.
Shock should not be the warrior's startle;
But beauty and gentleness are the warrior's treasure.
When man fights man, should there be bloodshed?
Wallowing in one's depression doesn't seem to be the way to
achieve true warriorship.
I enjoy fields of blooming warriors who chant the war cry.
I also enjoy warriors riding horses that never buck but smoothly
sail through enemy troops.

PART FIVE

ALL-VICTORIOUS

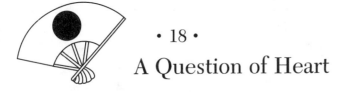

• 18 •

A Question of Heart

THE QUESTION that we're going to discuss tonight is a very simple one. It is a question of heart. As warriors, we should have a soft heart. That is what the world needs. The heart of warriorship is also fearlessness. Having a heart *at all* is based on being fearless and manifesting a sense of warriorship. When we talk about becoming a warrior, we are not talking about conducting *war*fare, but we're talking about manifesting fearlessness and gentleness that can save the world.

We have to be genuine, which means not having aggression and being true to oneself. In that way, we can build an enlightened society. Enlightened society cannot be built and cannot develop on the level of dreams or concepts. Enlightened society has to be real and good, honest and genuine.

A lot of us feel attacked by our own aggression and by our own misery and pain. But none of that particularly presents an obstacle to creating enlightened society. What we need, to begin with, is to develop kindness toward ourselves and then to develop kindness toward others. It sounds very simpleminded, which it is. At the same time, it is *very* difficult to practice.

I would like to keep our discussion very simple and direct. Pain causes a lot of chaos and resentment, and we have to overcome that. It is an extremely simple logic. Once we can overcome pain, we discover intrinsic joy, and we have less resentment toward the world and ourselves. By being here, naturally being here, we have less resentment. Resentment is not being here. We are somewhere else, because we are preoccupied with something else. When we are here, we are simply here—without resentment and without preoccupation. And by being here, we become cheerful. Let me see you smile. That's it! Good luck.

STUDENT: What should we do if people take advantage of our kindheartedness and use it against us? Most people feel that they can only give so much, but they also need to receive. We feel we can't give and give and give to people who just take and take and take.

DORJE DRADUL OF MUKPO: Give your goodness back to them. Let them glow. You have that much power. You can do it. You don't need to rely on anybody else's goodness. You have a resource already, which is your own goodness. You are already good, and you can actually transmit that goodness to others. In Buddhism, we call it *tathagatagarbha,* or buddha-nature.

Suppose you heard a talk about the heart. You might say, "Where is *my* heart? Do *I* have one?" Examine yourself and your state of being. You will find that you have the heart of goodness *in you.* You have it, and you'd better use it. One of the problems we have is feeling poverty-stricken. To overcome that, we have to be direct, and we have to trust ourselves. We are *not* poverty-stricken. If we are capable of smiling, we have goodness in us, always. Whether young or old, very old or very young, still, there are always possibilities of a smile. In fact, people do smile, at least three times a day. That is goodness. So keep smiling. Enjoy your being.

STUDENT: When you give a general prescription like "Be kind, smile, and be true to yourself," I can't help but think about women being abused and raped, about one class of people exploiting and oppressing other classes, or about people starving to death. On a world scale, I see incredible alienation, exploitation, and class oppression. How can what you're saying change the world?

DORJE DRADUL OF MUKPO: We can change the world, definitely. The problem is that we don't smile when chaos occurs to us. When chaos occurs, even within that chaos, we can smile, which cures confusion and resentment. Do you understand?

STUDENT: When you say to smile, are you saying that we should throw the hatred out?

DORJE DRADUL OF MUKPO: Absolutely. Yes. You got it.

STUDENT: Could you talk about the Tibetan legends concerning the Kingdom of Shambhala?

DORJE DRADUL OF MUKPO: Shambhala was an enlightened society that manifested nonaggression. Its geographic location was in the middle of Asia, in the middle, or the heart, of the Orient. The Shambhala society was able to transmute aggression into love. Consequently, everybody in Shambhala attained enlightenment, so they no longer needed to fight wars. Finally, the whole society, the whole country—including all the buildings—ceased to exist on the earthly plane. That is the story of Shambhala.

STUDENT: Do you think the Kingdom of Shambhala will manifest again on a worldwide scale as a golden or enlightened age?

DORJE DRADUL OF MUKPO: You bet.

STUDENT: Do you have any time frame for that—say, a hundred years or two hundred years from now?

193

DORJE DRADUL OF MUKPO: Right now. It is possible.

STUDENT: Many lamas have said it may happen within a hundred or two hundred years.

DORJE DRADUL OF MUKPO: That's speculation. It happens right now.

· 19 ·

The Mukpo Clan

GOOD MORNING, LADIES AND GENTLEMEN. I say good morning, even though it's evening, because as far as we are concerned, the sun always rises, and the sun is the source of brilliance. For the warriors of Shambhala, the sun is never a setting sun. This has nothing to do with cultural philosophy of any kind. The sun always shines because *you* always shine. You are shining at this moment. The sun is a symbol of that *ever glowing.*

Tonight, we're going further in our understanding and realization of the Shambhala principles. To begin with, we feel revulsion toward the setting-sun world. The setting sun is one's personal depression. Anything that you think is grossly unpleasant, or *yucky,* is connected with the setting-sun principle. We are trying to get out of that setting-sun world by trusting in ourselves and becoming warriors.

You have a head on your body, and when the head and the body are synchronized together, you realize that you are a real human being and a decent human being. In the Shambhala teachings, we call that having good head and shoulders. With that very ordinary experience of head and shoulders, you begin to smile.

When you realize that you don't have to separate mind and body, then you can eat properly, sleep properly, get your hair cut properly—do anything properly. You can experience tremendous sacredness in ordinary activities. What is ordinarily regarded as casual activity, we regard as the sacredness of Shambhala.

In traditional societies such as the Tibetan society I came from, you ride your horse, you pitch your tent, you make a fire. Whatever you do, it is done simply and directly. If you have to kill your enemy, you do so in the same spirit of simplicity and directness. Your enemy should die in your lap rather than being slaughtered off in the distance. And having killed your enemy, you're supposed to kiss the enemy. I don't know if you can understand this. In America, the white man just wiped out the Indians. There was no sense of sacred warfare. What I'm talking about is quite the opposite of that approach.

Last night, we talked about the importance of the warrior's smile. That is daringness. Whatever you do, you are not confused or intimidated. Like an eagle perched on a boulder, you fluff up your feathers with the demeanor of fearless dignity. Eating, walking, sleeping: you are not afraid to do anything. Please be decent. You don't have to be cowards anymore. Do you understand? For the warrior, fearlessness and love are the same. When you are in love, you are terrified at the same time. Nevertheless, you can develop love without terror and without horror.

The Shambhala flag represents the principles we're talking about tonight. The yellow disk is the sun, which symbolizes compassion. The surrounding white space is skillful means. White also represents wakefulness and yellow, wisdom. There are four stripes on the flag, which represent four stages in the warrior's understanding and attainment. The blue stripe represents inscrutability. The red represents the sense of outrageousness. The white stripe represents perkiness. Perky, in this case, is the sense that you're awake all the time. Last, the orange stripe represents

meekness. Meekness is humble modesty that brings together all of the Shambhala qualities that we have developed.

I have a personal flag or standard that incorporates the same principles. On this flag, the tiger represents meekness, the lion represents perkiness, the garuda represents outrageousness, and the dragon represents inscrutability. Going down one side of the flag, there are six black dots, which represent the six traditional clans of Tibet. All of the Tibetan clans practiced the disciplines of meek, perky, outrageous, and inscrutable. The six clans of Tibet are somewhat like Scottish clans, in that they represent the strength and dignity of family and the power of joining your identity together with others.

I am from the Mukpo clan. His Holiness Dilgo Khyentse Rinpoche and His Holiness the Sixteenth Gyalwa Karmapa also be-

197

long to this clan. The great Tibetan warrior Gesar of Ling was also from the Mukpo clan. Clan is a general way of relating to reality. Clan is a sense of how to rule the world and how to perceive the world at the same time. The heritage and benevolence of the Mukpo clan are my gift to you. Decency is the heritage of the Mukpos. In the past, the Mukpo clan tried to be decent, and we achieved decency altogether. Why not pass that decency down to you and the generations to come?

Please smile and please join our clan. Meek, perky, outrageous, and inscrutable are the way we work. It was, and it still is. I have been working with those principles since I came to the Western world, and now I am giving this treasure to each one of you.

There's nothing very much to say. By giving you this gift, it is both the closing of one door and the opening of another. I feel so relieved, so unburdened that you can share the Mukpo experience of helping others. My clan is yours, and I am so pleased that you are joining my clan. My clan has never deceived anybody. My clan shed *so much blood* in order to protect and maintain meek, perky, outrageous, and inscrutable. We worked so hard, ladies and gentlemen.

I didn't come to America to sit on a comfy cushion. I came here, you realize, to promote and to present everything that the Mukpo clan has gone through. It's real, sweethearts. It takes tremendous effort to be genuine and real, and tonight such effort is being shared with you. Warriorship is being handed over to you. I am giving you the heart of the warrior tradition. The Mukpos are not into having fake warriors, or double warriors, like in *Kagemusha.*[1] We are true, maybe too true. It is up to you, of course,

---

1. In Kurosawa's film *Kagemusha,* a Japanese lord dies, and his officials find a peasant who has an eerie resemblance to him. They train him and force him to take the lord's place. He successfully plays this role and fools everyone throughout much of the movie. The theme is similar to Mark Twain's *The Prince and the Pauper.*

but *we* never cheat. If we have to, we kill on the spot. If necessary, we would slice off a person's head without doubt, without confusion. Whatever the situation calls for, we are always true to ourselves. At the same time, tremendous joy and celebration take place. It is quite different from a wake. When somebody has died, at a wake, you might drink a lot to drown your sorrows—before the funeral. That is not the way of the Mukpos.

Shambhala means being true and honest at the same time. One thing you can be certain of: in the Shambhala world, nobody will be cheated, at all. If you keep a long face and hold on to your aggression, you will be punished by your own aggression. Otherwise, the Shambhala principles are quite cheerful! Thank you very much.

I

AUSPICIOUS COINCIDENCE
Wealth and Vision

The tiger has developed more stripes.
The lion has developed more mane.
Could the garuda fly further!
Is it possible that the dragon could resound deeper!
Could my ten years of being here be more!
Sometimes I feel I have been in North America 10,000 years;
Other times, maybe only ten seconds—
We grow young and old simultaneously.

We certainly appreciate what we have done,
What we have achieved, in ten kalpas[1] or ten seconds.
It is wondrous,
Shocking,
That you as the noble sangha
And I as the Vajra Master—
We grew old together.
Such a wonderful dharmic world would be impossible
If we never met each other.

We could say that the wise and the wicked have no time to rest.
Let us not indulge each other
In the ground, path and fruition of our journey.
Let us wake and join in the celebration,
And let us go further without rest.
In the name of the lineage and our forefathers,

1. A kalpa is a very long aeon, sometimes reckoned as 4,320 million years.

Let us hitch up our chubas fearlessly;
Let us bring about the dawn of tantra
Along with the Great Eastern Sun.

II

HAIKU

(excerpt)

All goes well.
Ki Ki—all goes worthywhile—So So!
I take pride in our expedition.
Since my mother left me without her fur chuba
I decided always to be chubaless,
A warrior without wearing clothes, walking in the cold.
My mother and my guru have agreed on this principle,
So now I am furless, clothesless.
On the other hand I remained a king,
Sitting on a throne with a self-snug smile.
If I never had my heritage,
This never would have happened:
Thanks to Gesar
And anybody related to the Mukpo family
Who has had the delicious meal of the Mongolian meat-eaters.
Good dish,
Solid gold brocade,
Genuine suit of armor,
Riding on a white horse into battle—

We take pride in all of those.
Ki Ki So So!
Ki Ki So So to Lady Jane!
Ki Ki So So to my white horse!
Ki Ki So So: we are the warriors without ego!
Om svabhava-shuddah sarva-dharmah svabhava-shuddho 'ham[2]
Ki Ki So So!

2. A traditional Buddhist mantra, or religious chant, that invokes the nontheistic principles of emptiness and egolessness. It means "All dharmas or phenomena are pure in nature; I am pure in nature."

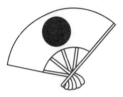

· 20 ·

Beyond Depression

OCCASIONALLY, we may have difficulty expressing ourselves or difficulty understanding the realities of human nature.
We may feel inadequate, thinking that there's something we don't
know. We think there's some knowledge we should acquire. In
that situation, the emphasis on learning is an obstacle. Why don't
we wake up without learning? Why don't we cheer up without
learning?

The real problem is that we cannot work with our depression.
We might say that depression is good: when we are depressed, we
begin to see the other shore. We can empathize with others, and
we can see the need for an alternative. Yet when we are depressed, we are unable to transcend neurosis. Let us give up depression. Let us literally give up depression.

Then we can smile beautifully, utterly, extraordinarily. Ladies
and gentlemen, why do we have to wallow in the mud? We don't
deserve that. We don't deserve to wallow in a pile of excrement.
Why don't we wake ourselves up! And smile at the same time!

We are capable of smiling. Let us not become dutiful oxen.
Let us not become obedient worms. Let us not become the worst

of the worst. I know that sometimes the brilliance of going beyond your depression is *so* terrifying, but nonetheless, you have to do it. Your cowardice will provide bravery at the same time. When you feel so cowardly and afraid, it is equal to when you see a terrible darkness: you see brilliance at the same time. Please come and join us with a smile. You can do it! It has been done, and you are capable of doing so. Thank you. Please ask questions.

STUDENT: Could you explain a little more what you meant by cheering up or waking up without having to learn?

DORJE DRADUL OF MUKPO: You tell me. What do you think?

STUDENT: Is it that we become too preoccupied with getting somewhere as opposed to just cheering up right on the spot?

DORJE DRADUL OF MUKPO: Yes, that's right. That's perfectly right. But there are some problems. What are the problems? Please tell us.

STUDENT: I suppose that, if you always take the approach that you must learn something more in order to cheer up or to wake up, all you're doing is setting up habitual patterns for yourself.

DORJE DRADUL OF MUKPO: That's right. Thank you very much. At this point, you are a child of Shambhala, and I'm proud of you.

STUDENT: Sir, did you say that depression is good and then say that we have to get rid of depression?

DORJE DRADUL OF MUKPO: Not quite get rid of depression *per se*. We can actually stand on the platform of depression. It's like this chair that I'm sitting on. A long time ago, it was made by people who were depressed. Now, we have flipped the coin. This particular chair is now a Shambhala chair, a Shambhala throne. So we are not trapped in depression. Ça va?

STUDENT: Is there some kind of wisdom behind the depression, and we get depressed because . . .

DORJE DRADUL OF MUKPO: Not wisdom *behind,* but wisdom in front. Wisdom is *there.* R-r-r-r-right now!

STUDENT: Then, why do we get depressed?

DORJE DRADUL OF MUKPO: You don't. People talk about miracles. Miracles don't occur, but at the same time, they occur. Miracles are worked on the spot, r-r-right on the spot. It makes us smile, and we begin to realize that reality is not a source of confusion and solemnness.

STUDENT: Sir, is it not possible to be cheerful and to still feel a full range of emotions: sadness, perhaps anger, all those feelings? When you say "Cheer up," that doesn't wipe out the emotions, does it?

DORJE DRADUL OF MUKPO: When we begin to see the Great Eastern Sun, we don't forget the setting sun. When we learn A, we don't forget Z. There is a possibility of bringing Z into A. Do you understand?

STUDENT: I hope I do. In this sense, that . . .

DORJE DRADUL OF MUKPO: You don't have any *hope.* You just do it.

STUDENT: But to feel different emotions . . .

DORJE DRADUL OF MUKPO: You don't have any *feel.*

STUDENT: You don't feel?

DORJE DRADUL OF MUKPO: You just do it.

STUDENT: Uh, but . . . can't you feel and . . .

DORJE DRADUL OF MUKPO: No, no, no, no, nonononono-noNO. You don't dabble in anything. You don't dabble in anything.

STUDENT: Well, an example might be that you see something very sad—say, the death of a child. That can be sad. Isn't it reasonable to feel—can't you . . .

DORJE DRADUL OF MUKPO: No.

STUDENT: Do it?

DORJE DRADUL OF MUKPO: No. We are talking about *genuineness*. Genuine on the *spot*. R-r-r-real genuine on the spot.

STUDENT: Suppose you're crying?

DORJE DRADUL OF MUKPO: You don't cry. You can cry *because* you did not cry. It's *on the spot*. Come on! Say something more.

STUDENT: What about revulsion?

DORJE DRADUL OF MUKPO: Because of that, you feel revolt-sion.

STUDENT: Because of what? Because of the feeling or the event?

DORJE DRADUL OF MUKPO: You are never revolted.

STUDENT: Never?

DORJE DRADUL OF MUKPO: Never! [*Burps. Audience laughter.*]

STUDENT [*laughing*]: Thank you, sir.

DORJE DRADUL OF MUKPO: Thank you! OK, at this point, we should probably adjourn. When the warriors of Shambhala meet together, sometimes we close our gathering by singing a very cheerful song, which is called the anthem of Shambhala. I hope you'll join in, and thank you very much, everybody.

ANTHEM

In heaven the turquoise dragon thunders,
The tiger's lightning flashes abroad.
The lion's mane spreads turquoise clouds,
Garuda spans the threefold world.

Fearless the warriors of Shambhala,
Majestic the Rigdens[1] on vajra[2] thrones.
The Sakyong[3] king joins heaven and earth.
The Sakyongwangmo harvests peace.

The trumpet of fearlessness resounds,
The all-victorious banner flies.
Temporal and spiritual glory expand.
Rejoice, the Great Eastern Sun arises!

---

1. The kings of Shambhala.

2. (Tib. *dorje*.) Adamantine or having the qualities of a diamond. *Vajra* refers to the basic indestructible nature of wisdom and enlightenment.

3. *Sakyong* and *Sakyongwangmo* are titular names of the rulers of Shambhala. The term *Sakyong* means "Earth Protector"; the *Sakyongwangmo* is the Earth Protector Lady.

The Great Eastern Sun
The Dot in Space

FOR THE LAST TIME, I'd like to say good morning, ladies and gentlemen. I would like to close with a discussion of daringness and warriorship. Daringness is based on being genuine within oneself. It is a very important principle, maybe the most important. It is the principle of nondeception.

Deception occurs first in oneself, and then deception is spread to others. Deceitfulness is one of the main obstacles to realizing the Shambhala principles. Whether one is eating, walking, or sleeping, whatever we do has the potential for deception. Because of deception, we are unable to see the dot in space. The dot in space is pure and clear, altogether unwavering. That dot in space is the way we hold ourselves upright. It is the Great Eastern Sun. The Great Eastern Sun is the dot in space.

All the variations of enlightened Shambhala society that we have talked about are the dot in space. They are based on not deceiving anybody and appreciating oneself at the same time. Being kind to oneself and therefore being capable of extending kindness to others both arise from the dot in space. The dot in space is a manifestation of your sanity. It is almost a ringing in your ears. Sometimes when you are going about your business, something goes *ding* in your ears. That is the dot in space. It is a reminder, and it is that which makes you smile. It is that which makes you glance around or look over your shoulder. That is the dot in space.

Who are they? Where are they? That's the dot in space![1] Inquisitiveness is the dot in space. Curiosity is the dot in space. Any question that comes into your state of being is the dot in space, always. One should not regard one's world as a boring world. There is always *Ah-ah!* There is always a spark. There is always a smile. There is always a cry, as well. That is the dot in space. That is why you are here, all of you.

I have experienced this myself. It is a personal experience. I'm not presenting fiction or philosophy. That which makes you gasp *Ah-ah!* is the dot in space. That which makes you *smile* is the dot in space.

STUDENT: Sir, when I'm lost in thought and something brings me back to a sense of self-awareness—in that moment that I wake from my thoughts or my depression or whatever I'm feeling, there doesn't seem to be any quality other than the awakeness. Sometimes it's pretty ho-hum. You make it sound very exciting.

DORJE DRADUL OF MUKPO: That awakeness is the dot in space. Inspired or not inspired: both are the dot in space. As long as you come back, that's fine. You have a long face: ohhh. You are beaming with a smile: ahh! Both are the dot in space. As long as you see the brilliance of the Great Eastern Sun, everything is all right.

1. I believe that the author is doing a takeoff here on a phrase connected with a television series or a film, but I haven't been able to identify the source of the reference.

If you can maintain a sense of humor, that will dispel deception, but we don't have any insurance policies here. You just have to keep going. For example, the *lohans* were great Indian saints and very great meditators. They were very serious people, in some sense. Within that, however, you can see that they were constantly laughing while they sat in meditation. That is what we are talking about.

I would like to leave all of you with one last reminder: when you are in a serious mood, smile, with Shambhala vision. The sitting practice of meditation is *very* important for you. *Just sit,* as you are instructed to do. I'm so pleased by your composure. Beyond that, the main point is to care for this world and also to have a sense of humor. Thank you very much.

Epilogue

IT HAS BEEN MORE THAN TEN YEARS since my father passed into *parinirvana.* In that time, many people have tried to fathom what he was about and what he meant as a historical figure, an individual, a Buddhist teacher, and a Shambhala warrior. As time passes, the heart and body of what he taught has become increasingly powerful. More and more people appreciate his compassionate demeanor and his overwhelming commitment to helping others.

My father is recognized as a pioneer in the transmission of Buddhism to the West. As such, one of his contributions is the translation and introduction of Buddhism into a context that Westerners can understand. However, if his life is looked at in more detail, it becomes evident that perhaps his greatest gift to the world is his unique presentation of the Shambhala tradition of warriorship.

Growing up with Chögyam Trungpa Rinpoche as my father, I lived in a Shambhala household. We practiced Buddhism, but the basic environment was Shambhalian. As is clearly stated in this book, understanding the wisdom of Shambhala is understanding basic human dignity. There are set principles and practices in Shambhala, but the root of the teachings is simply how to be a decent human being, how to live in a harmonious way.

The wisdom of Shambhala has been gathered for many centuries. This wisdom shows that there is a path, a way to live, and points to how the world works. We do not need to search endlessly or to concoct our own recipes for the meaning of life. Many

Shambhala warriors have realized the basic rhythm, the basic energy of their lives. Our duty, our joy, and our fascination with life all come together when we are able to touch that energy, understanding that is it the dignity of all humankind. This is not a celestial or otherworldly power. If we lead our lives appreciating both the mundane and the extraordinary qualities, holding them both equally, without preference, with a gentle hand and compassionate gaze, we have discovered what being a human being, what being a Shambhala warrior, is.

I hope that people are able to read this book many times so that it can soak into their bones. I hope its meaning can have an influence on how they conduct their lives. The power of Shambhala is not so much that we "get the idea" or that with a quick glance we understand everything. Rather, we begin to realize that these simple teachings take time to be understood and even more time to be absorbed into our hearts.

In and of itself, the Shambhala vision is not overly complicated or difficult. Often we see it and say, "Oh, I know that." It feels like something very familiar to us. The real challenge is letting these principles penetrate our being and not letting arrogance and depression consume us. The Shambhala warrior knows that life can be simple. Yet these straightforward teachings have a profound effect. They are not theoretical spiritual exercises: they are pragmatic methods to help people raise their children, develop art, or run their own coffee shops. Through the years, the practical element of these teachings has become more and more powerful.

Often the Dorje Dradul would say that these teachings were not his alone but that he was a representative of their sanity and dignity. In a confusing and speedy world, he felt it was his duty to offer them for individuals who were willing to listen. He would say that the Shambhala vision was much bigger than he was and that he would not live forever. Others would have to assume responsibility for carrying out these teachings. I think he would be very proud of, and delighted by, how people have taken his words to heart and tried to understand and live according to them.

Many aspects of the Shambhala world have been expounded and written about since that early time when he first presented them to a small handful of people. From those earliest talks, the Dorje Dradul went on to present the Shambhala teachings to thousands of interested listeners. Many students and admirers of the Dorje Dradul try to conduct their lives according to these principles. We refer to this as creating enlightened society.

In the early 1970s, people wanted esoteric Buddhist teachings. They were rather puzzled when the Dorje Dradul presented instead seemingly simpleminded teachings on how to live in a decent way. Now, hundreds of thousands of people realize that those simple, practical instructions are extraordinarily useful.

In the past twenty-five years, the Shambhala teachings have taken root. Since the passing of the Dorje Dradul, many people have participated in the Shambhala Training program, which continues to grow and expand. It is inspiring to see such a diverse group of people practicing and living their lives according to these teachings—people of many faiths in many different parts of the world.

As I have now inherited my father's work, and particularly the responsibility for propagating Shambhala vision, I am very grateful to Carolyn Rose Gimian for her diligence, resourcefulness, and intelligence in assembling this material.

Please enjoy this book just as you would enjoy sitting outside early in the morning, soaking up the warm rays of the Great Eastern Sun.

The Sakyong, Jamgon Mipham Rinpoche

Afterword

SHAMBHALA: The Sacred Path of the Warrior was first published in 1984. Although its author, Chögyam Trungpa, was one of the best-known Tibetan Buddhist teachers in the West, *Shambhala* is not a book about Buddhism. While drawing on the heritage of Buddhist meditation practice, it presents a unique path for awakening based on the Shambhala teachings of warriorship.

Chögyam Trungpa, Dorje Dradul of Mukpo, died on April 4, 1987, in Halifax, Nova Scotia. Between his death and this writing, more than a dozen books by him on various aspects of the Buddhist path have been published, using the audiotapes of his lectures as source material. However, this is the first new book by him on the Shambhala teachings. *Great Eastern Sun: The Wisdom of Shambhala* was the Dorje Dradul's provisional title for his first book on the Shambhala teachings, but it was later changed. However, it was the perfect title for the present volume. A friend of mine, Rick Fields, once said that Chögyam Trungpa was the master of the delayed punch line. This is certainly one of those times.

Although *Great Eastern Sun* is not primarily a book about Buddhism, its author was, as noted above, one of the great Tibetan Buddhist teachers of the twentieth century. For readers unfamiliar with his life and work, some biographical information may be helpful.

BACKGROUND

Chögyam Trungpa Rinpoche was born in 1939 in a cowshed on a high plateau in eastern Tibet, in a region where many people have never seen a tree. While still a babe in arms, he was recognized as an incarnate lama, or *tulku*. With his parents' blessings, he was taken to the Surmang monasteries, where he was enthroned as the abbot and the eleventh Trungpa Tulku, or the eleventh incarnation of the Trungpa lineage. Trungpa Rinpoche's enthronement was conducted by His Holiness the sixteenth Gyalwa Karmapa, the head of the Karma Kagyü lineage, who figures prominently in this book.[1] At a later date, he was given the name *Chögyam*, which means "Dharma Ocean" or "Ocean of Teachings." *Rinpoche* is an honorific title, which means "precious jewel."

Trungpa Rinpoche's root guru, or main teacher, was a great ecumenical scholar and teacher, Jamgon Kongtrul of Sechen. Among Trungpa Rinpoche's spiritual mentors, two other figures were of particular importance: Khenpo Gangshar and His Holiness Dilgo Khyentse Rinpoche, who also receives mention in this volume.[2] Like many of the great lamas of his generation, Chögyam Trungpa was forced by the invasion of the Chinese to flee Tibet in 1959. He tells the story of his escape in *Born in Tibet,* his first book, published in 1966. Upon successfully reaching India, he was appointed by His Holiness the Dalai Lama to be the spiritual adviser to the Young Lamas' School in Dalhousie, and he remained in India until 1963.

In 1963, Trungpa Rinpoche traveled to England, where he became the first Tibetan to study at Oxford University, in St. Anthony's College. He also was quite proud to be the first Tibetan ever to become a British subject. He studied the English language in Oxford; attended courses on philosophy, history, and religion; took up flower arranging; began to write poetry; and attracted his first Western disciples. In 1966, he was given a center for the

1. See "Overcoming Physical Materialism," "The King of Basic Goodness," "Attaining the Higher Realms," "The Big No," "Helping Others," and "The Mukpo Clan."

2. See "Mirrorlike Wisdom" and "The Mukpo Clan."

practice and study of meditation in Scotland, which he named Samye Ling, or Samye Place, Samye having been the first monastery established in Tibet. Although many Westerners came to study with him there and he was able to present an exposition of the Buddhist teachings, he felt a growing dissatisfaction with the spiritual climate that surrounded him.

In 1968, he visited the Buddhist kingdom of Bhutan, at the invitation of the queen mother. While there, he conducted a ten-day retreat at Tagtsang—the holy cave where the founder of Buddhism in Tibet, Guru Rinpoche (or Padmasambhava), meditated before entering Tibet. After several days in retreat, Trungpa Rinpoche had a vision of Guru Rinpoche and received[3] a sacred practice text, *The Sadhana of Mahamudra*, which is connected with overcoming spiritual, psychological, and physical materialism—the three lords of materialism who rule Western society in this dark age.

Soon after returning to England, while behind the wheel of a car, Trungpa Rinpoche blacked out and crashed into a building. He survived but was paralyzed on his left side. He remarked on this event as a pivotal occurrence in his life. It woke him to the dangers of self-deception and convinced him to remove his monastic robes and become a lay practitioner—thus removing a layer of distance between himself and Western students.

Shortly after this, he proposed to Diana Judith Pybus, a young woman of sixteen who became his wife, much to the consternation of both her family and Trungpa Rinpoche's Tibetan colleagues. Life was extremely difficult for Trungpa Rinpoche and Diana at Samye Ling. There was anger and confusion, not only about the marriage but about the general direction in which Trungpa Rin-

---

3. In Tibetan Buddhism, there is a tradition of certain teachers' uncovering or finding texts that were buried in the subconscious mind—or some might say, in space—by Padmasambhava. These teachings are considered to be "received" rather than composed.

poche was headed. Some did not like the intimacy that Trungpa Rinpoche was establishing with Westerners and felt, I imagine, bewilderment and concern that he was heading into dangerous and uncharted territory. Students at Samye Ling took sides in the conflict, and it ended very badly, with Trungpa Rinpoche and Diana leaving for North America, somewhat at her urging. Without her support during this period, it is hard to imagine that Rinpoche would have survived the ordeal.

After a brief stay in Montreal, Chögyam and Diana Mukpo were admitted to the United States and went to live at a rural meditation center in Vermont, to which Rinpoche gave the name Tail of the Tiger.[4] From there, his buddha activity fanned out across the continent, at a dizzying pace. Between 1970, when he arrived in North America, and April 4, 1987, when he died in Halifax, Nova Scotia, Trungpa Rinpoche gave more than five thousand recorded talks (to audiences that together number in the hundreds of thousands); founded innumerable organizations, including more than one hundred Buddhist centers for the practice and study of meditation; and attracted more than three thousand committed Western students who became advanced practitioners of the vajrayana, or tantric, teachings of Tibetan Buddhism. He taught many thousands of people to meditate, and his books have sold in the millions of copies in more than a dozen languages.

He was a pioneer, one of the first Tibetan Buddhist teachers in North America, preceding by some years, and indeed facilitating, the later visits by His Holiness the Karmapa, His Holiness Khyentse Rinpoche, His Holiness the Dalai Lama, and many others. In the United States, he found a spiritual kinship with many of the Zen masters who were already presenting Buddhist meditation. In the very early days, he particularly connected with Suzuki

4. It was later renamed Karme Chöling, or Dharma Place of Action, by His Holiness the sixteenth Karmapa.

Roshi, the founder of the Zen Center in San Francisco. In later years, he was close with Kobun Chino Roshi and Bill Kwong Roshi in northern California and with Maezumi Roshi, the founder of the Los Angeles Zen Center.

Trungpa Rinpoche was also an ecumenical leader. In 1974, he founded the Naropa Institute in Boulder, Colorado. The institute attracted religious and spiritual teachers from numerous disciplines. For example, the first summer at Naropa, Rinpoche invited Ram Dass, a very popular exponent of Hindu spirituality, to teach there. His book, *Be Here Now,* was all the rage in the early seventies. Buddhist teachers of many traditions and lineages lectured at Naropa, and Trungpa Rinpoche also initiated a Christian-Buddhist conference through Naropa that brought together contemplative practitioners from both of these great world religions.

Chögyam Trungpa's ecumenicism was cultural as well as religious. He attracted poets, playwrights, dancers, musicians, photographers, painters—artists of all sorts, some famous, some obscure, many very talented. His legacy is visible in the programs that showcase the arts at Naropa.

Early black-and-white videotapes of Trungpa Rinpoche's lectures at Naropa provide us with a window of sorts back in time. In the early to mid-1970s, many of Chögyam Trungpa's Buddhist students and probably a majority of those interested in alternative approaches to spirituality were young, unkempt, longhaired hippies who had rejected the mainstream of American society. Many had radical political ideas and were Vietnam War protesters or aspiring Hindu yogis with long, matted hair and malas, or rosaries, around their necks chanting *om.* If you view tapes from this era, Trungpa Rinpoche looks quite normal. While not sporting a suit and tie, he was dressed in attractive and colorful silk and cotton shirts that today would be quite elegant. In contrast, shots that pan the audience reveal a crowd of twenty-something flower children—a notable contrast to today's staid yet trendy, well-heeled, and often middle-aged meditators. Some of the emphasis in the Shambhala teachings presented here on proprieties of dress, the importance of a clean-cut approach, the value of personal discipline, and acceptance of basic hierarchy can partly be ascribed to the "raw" material that the author was working with and the tenor of the times.

THE ORIGINS OF THE SHAMBHALA TRAINING

Given all that he had already done—in just six years in North America—it was certainly enterprising and rather surprising when, in 1977, Chögyam Trungpa launched a completely new program, Shambhala Training, to present the practice of meditation to a broad audience with diverse spiritual and religious affiliations. The Shambhala teachings and the creation of the Shambhala world were his deep and abiding passion for the last ten years of his life.

His interest in Shambhala did not arise suddenly. His connection dated from his training in Tibet, where he studied various texts related to this tradition. In fact, when he was fleeing the Chinese across the Himalayas, he was working on a manuscript about Shambhala, which was lost during the escape. However, not much was said about Shambhala during his early years in North America. Then, in 1976, it burst onto the scene: he began receiving texts[5] related to the Shambhala teachings and began to introduce his senior students to this path. From that grew the idea of an expansive program of practice and study to be presented to a Western audience on a large scale.

With the help of many of his senior Buddhist students, Chögyam Trungpa presented the Shambhala teachings through a series of weekend programs, the five levels of the Shambhala

---

5. See note 3 in this afterword for an explanation of "received" texts.

Training program. The first four levels were taught by Trungpa Rinpoche's students, with his chief student and Western dharma heir, the Vajra Regent Ösel Tendzin, presenting the fourth level. The early levels introduced the practice of meditation and the fundamental teachings of Shambhala warriorship. For the first six years, Trungpa Rinpoche taught the fifth and final level himself, and it is these talks that form the body of this book.

The exposition of the Shambhala teachings also led Chögyam Trungpa to Nova Scotia, one of the Maritime provinces on the east coast of Canada. He found a seat for his Buddhist work in Boulder, Colorado, where he established the Naropa Institute and Vajradhatu, the international headquarters for the network of Buddhist centers he founded. But with the introduction of the Shambhala teachings, he began to look for a new seat and, I think, a place where the Shambhala world would flourish. He found that spot in this unlikely corner of the continent. One of the last great projects of his life was to move his home and the seat of his work to Halifax, the capital of Nova Scotia. Today, Nova Scotia is the headquarters of Shambhala International, the umbrella organization for both Vajradhatu and Shambhala Training, the Buddhist and the Shambhala containers for his teachings.

CONTROVERSY AND GENUINENESS

In this brief exposition of his life's work, it would be an oversight not to mention that Chögyam Trungpa's life was also controversial. Tremendous movement characterized Trungpa Rinpoche's life; tremendous energy infused his teaching. As well, his own life was an example of the blending of religious and secular activity that he taught. He was known for his love of drink and women, and the progress of his life was characterized by a number of powerful explosions. The communist Chinese invasion of his country exploded him—and many others—out of Tibet. His accident was another eruption, exploding him out of his robes. Troubles at Samye Ling exploded him out of Britain and brought him to North America. Finally, controversy dogged Trungpa Rinpoche's reputation even after death, due to the tragic circumstances surrounding the death of the Vajra Regent Ösel Tendzin, from complications of HIV. As a result, some Western Buddhists have attacked Trungpa Rinpoche, his teachings, his followers, and his reputation.

Certainly, during his lifetime, controversy did not bother Chögyam Trungpa. In fact, he welcomed it. His sense of integrity did not come from outside judgments, and he always felt it was better to let things come out into the open. He was not trying to hide anything.

Unconventional behavior by presumably enlightened teachers is sometimes defended as the teachers' way of communicating with the samsaric, or confused, world of the students with whom they work. This might be said of Trungpa Rinpoche. I don't think, however, that he would have used such an argument to explain his behavior. I remember his interchange with a reporter from the *Boulder Daily Camera*, who, in an interview around 1983, asked him about his alleged sexual promiscuity. He replied that, regardless of his personal relationships, he had a love affair with all of his students. He had an extraordinary passion for human beings and a rather outrageous capability to see us from the inside out. He never preached from afar. This was one of his greatest strengths.

In the 1970s and 1980s, he reached out to thousands who couldn't relate to a traditional approach to religion, yet were starved for spirituality. His teachings still have that quality of being genuine and guileless. While editing this volume, I experienced such relief to hear a spiritual teacher talking about any and every topic without any pretense of religiosity.

About five years ago, the Shambhala Archives (of which I was then the director) was just beginning the transfer of some of the above-mentioned half-inch reel-to-reel videotapes recorded at the Naropa Institute in the early seventies. I sat in on the transfer of a panel discussion on death and dying, where Chögyam Trungpa joined two Western therapists talking about death. One of the therapists, now a leading Buddhist authority on death and dying, was very self-serious and solemn during the discussion. She seemed to be adopting the posture of a wise, caring person talking about a very important, serious subject like death. Then, at the very end of the reel, after the discussion was finished and the participants felt "off-camera," this young woman was shown on camera asking Trungpa Rinpoche for a cigarette. Suddenly, as she smoked her cigarette, she became young, carefree, and sexy. Rinpoche didn't change at all. It was interesting.

Trungpa Rinpoche had an incredible knack for saying things that people are always thinking but are afraid to talk about. He didn't pull his punches. There are many examples of this in the present volume, some humorous, some shocking, some heartrending. I hope the editing has done him justice in this regard.

His command of the English language would have been impressive for a native speaker; it was quite extraordinary for a gentleman from Tibet. His choice of English terms to define key concepts in the Buddhist teachings and his rich and metaphoric use of the English language in his books have to a great extent defined the vocabulary of Buddhism in America and helped to provide its poetic voice. His understanding of the Western mind is uncanny. Now, more than ten years after his death, those qualities still make him unique among spiritual teachers in the West. This is one of the many reasons that, privately, *everyone* reads him, although not everyone admits it.

Chögyam Trungpa was a teacher for many times, not just for the generation to whom he delivered his teachings. As he says over and over in this book, what he truly cared about was benefiting others. I hope that his teachings will be recognized for the wisdom they contain.

GREAT EASTERN SUN: THE WISDOM OF SHAMBHALA

SOURCE MATERIALS AND STRUCTURE

Except for two chapters that are based on public talks, this book is based entirely on weekend seminars given by Trungpa Rinpoche in Level Five of the Shambhala Training program. The programs that formed the basis for the book were given in New York City; Boston, Massachusetts; Boulder, Colorado; Berkeley, California; and Vancouver, British Columbia. The audience for each program was usually between 150 and 200 students who had completed four training seminars, also conducted as weekend programs. The Level Five would begin with a Friday night talk. During the day on Saturday and Sunday, periods of sitting and walking meditation would be interspersed with individual interviews and group discussions conducted by assistant directors who were senior students of the author. The concluding event each day would be a talk in the evening by the author. Following the final talk of the weekend on Sunday, students would receive a diploma and pin to signify their graduation from the program, and there was usually a reception with food and drink, often accompanied by poetry readings, singing, and toasts—and occasionally other events such as a calligraphy demonstration by the Dorje Dradul. The chapters in the book are generally grouped together in two, threes, or fours—mostly threes—corresponding to the three talks given by the author in each program. I have given every chapter and grouping a title, drawn from the content of the talks on which they are based.

At the time that the talks were given, the title of every Level Five seminar was "Open Sky/Primordial Stroke." The talks in the program were based on a simple threefold logic, one logic for each talk: trust, renunciation, and letting go. Thus, from one point of view, almost all the talks in this book are about one of these three topics, although each talk is also unique. No attempt was made to mask repetitiveness in the content, but I hope that, nevertheless, readers find the material of interest. In the editor's preface, I have offered some possible approaches to exploring the redundancy of the material.

Some of the material in *Great Eastern Sun* also appeared in *Shambhala.* In the first volume, it was generally used in quite a different context, so I have not been shy about allowing the occasional reedit and reuse of material in *Great Eastern Sun.* In preparing transcripts as source materials for this book, I found that the audiotapes of talks that were the most powerful and poignant were often the worst-quality recordings. I don't know why that is the case; I merely report it. Most of the talks on which this book is based have been unavailable to people since the time they were given, some almost twenty years ago. Many of the tapes were never transcribed, and unlike most of the author's other Shambhala presentations, this material was not widely studied. It is a pleasure to return it to the world. In one case, the last talk of a seminar was missing, and I sent out a call over the Internet to the members of the Shambhala community to locate this talk. Although given in Boston, the only known copy of the recording turned up in the local office of Shambhala Training in Boulder, Colorado. In another case, the audiotapes of an entire Level Five given in Chicago were missing and could not be located.

Readers may want to hear some of the recordings for themselves. I would recommend this, although the poor quality of some does not allow for their general release. Tapes of some of the original seminars can be purchased in their entirety from Kalapa Recordings. (For information about contacting the publisher, see p. 249.)

For some, it may be of interest to know that the Dorje Dradul's own study material for these talks was often the Tibetan text *Moonbeams of Mahamudra*, by Tagpo Tashi Namgyal. An English translation was published in 1986 by Shambhala Publications and is now out of print.

EDITORIAL DECISIONS

I had three principles that guided me in the editing of the manuscript. They were not to change or omit anything simply because (1) I didn't understand it, (2) I didn't agree with it, or (3) it made me uncomfortable. There are many things in the book that I don't understand, a few things that I don't agree with, and certainly places in the book that make me uncomfortable. Thinking about it, I realized that this was a mark of Chögyam Trungpa, the Dorje Dradul, the man and his teachings: he often makes us very uncomfortable. It seems to be part of the genuineness.

There was some profanity in the original manuscript, which I eventually removed. The Dorje Dradul never used profanity in a habitual fashion. He used it deliberately and powerfully. However, if the author were alive today, I don't think that he would want swear words in print in the context of a book clearly meant for a large and diverse reading public. During his lifetime, he certainly favored a formal approach to the written word. Fairly early on in the editing of the book, I had occasion to speak with Mrs. Diana Mukpo, the wife of the Dorje Dradul, and I mentioned the issue of profanity to her, especially the use of the f-word in several chapters. I remember that she said, "Oh dear!" in her most regal, English fashion, and then laughed.

Some of the talks on which this book is based were quite rigorous expositions of the Shambhala wisdom, and I have tried to respect their rigor. Others were more atmospheric, and I have tried to communicate the atmosphere. I have tried to retain as much of the humor as I could. In most cases, answers to questions have been either incorporated into the body of a chapter or omitted. In a few cases, a question or an interchange was left in dialogue format. Audio recordings of some events included the closing ceremonies, toasts, and other details mentioned above. Occasionally, those were incorporated into a chapter. This was not done primarily to communicate the atmosphere *then*. Rather, I have tried to let the nowness of events speak out. The reader will have to judge whether this attempt has been successful or not.

Sometimes, editing from the spoken word to a written text is mainly a matter of adding punctuation and correcting grammar. That approach can work well if the original language was being chanted or the recitation was a form of poetry. But for most of the material in this book, I took another approach to try to grapple with the nuances of meaning and expression. I didn't want to ignore the intonation and emphasis put on different words or the rhythm and melody of the author's speech, which make his language so alive and rich. I did a fair bit of pruning of the language in this book. Most people include a lot of extra words in their speech, many of which are de-emphasized when they talk, but which become large and glaring on the page. So although I tried to respect both the letter and the sense of the original, many words were cut back. I have worked very hard not to put many words into the author's mouth in this book. Occasionally, I felt that I had no choice but to add a word or phrase, so that readers would not be unnecessarily confused. The end result, I hope, captures the lithic quality of the Dorje Dradul's speech. He uses words in ways that are so concrete, as well as alive, that you feel you can almost hold them in your hand.

I have tried to respect the author's voice in this book. For some, it will seem raw, although I hope that it will also seem immediate and alive. *Great Eastern Sun* is being presented more than twelve years after his death. Liberties I took with the first book I don't feel are appropriate now. Some readers may find the voice and the approach to content in this book a contrast to *Shambhala: The Sacred Path of the Warrior.* In that volume, the author's personality was downplayed, in keeping with his instructions to me about the kind of book that he wanted. For the present volume, I didn't edit out the outrageous, humorous, and disturbing qualities that made the author the powerful, magnetic, and controversial teacher that he was. I haven't taken anything out purely because it might be shocking, quirky, or controversial. I hope this will make it harder to expropriate these teachings as food for New Age dogma.

Editing, at its best, is like being a midwife—helping to bring the expression of an idea or an emotion into the world but not confusing it for one's own achievement. In this case, the midwife felt that she was staring into the womb of space, witnessing the birth of the primordial dot.

This book was edited in Nova Scotia, the last place that the Dorje Dradul called home. Most of the work on the book was done in retreat in a little house grandly named Trident Mountain House on Tatamagouche Mountain in the autumn of 1997 and the spring of 1998. During one of his early visits to Nova Scotia, the Dorje Dradul passed through the town of Tatamagouche and stopped for a meal at the Balmoral Inn. After lunch, all of us in his party went for a walk in a field behind the restaurant that slopes down through alders to the harbor. We were less than ten miles from the current site of the rural practice center, Dorje Denma Ling, which the Shambhala community established in 1990. It was very close to this location that I worked on the book, a pure coincidence that pleases me.

I do not think that this book would have taken its present form anywhere else. Nova Scotia provided the air, the atmosphere, of simplicity and open space in which this book took shape. And now, some twelve years after his death, this place still echoes with

the mind of the Dorje Dradul, projecting his uncomfortable, un-compromising, and vast sanity. If that quality is not apparent in this manuscript, then the failure is mine. Certainly, it pervades his teachings.

ACKNOWLEDGMENTS AND DEDICATION

There are many people to thank. Fifteen years ago, Robert Walker and Rachel Anderson prepared some of the original transcripts of talks used in this book. Thanks to both of them. Tingdzin Ötro transcribed many others during the winter of 1997 and checked the earlier transcriptions. Thank you, Ting. The staff of the Shambhala Archives provided copies of tapes and transcripts that were the basis for the book, gave me the long-term loan of audio equipment, and were supportive in many other ways. Thanks to James Hoagland, Donna Holm, Gordon Kidd, Judith Smith, and Alexis Shotwell for this. The publisher at Shambhala Publications, Samuel Bercholz, and my editor there, Emily Hilburn Sell, both provided motivation and feedback. I thank them as well for their ongoing commitment to publishing the teachings of Chögyam Trungpa. Thanks also to Hazel Bercholz at Shambhala Publications for the design of the book and Jonathan Green, Amy Allin, Jenn Martin, and Jennifer Pursley for helping in other ways. Particular thanks to John Rockwell, Scott Wellenbach, and Larry Mermelstein of the Nalanda Translation Committee for the translation of the author's note cards and for providing Tibetan script of the poems that open and close the book. As well, a thank-you to the photographers who contributed illustrative material to the book; to Peter Volz, Eric Schneider, Eve Rosenthal, and Robin Kornman for help with several entries in the glossary; to Susan Cohan for excellent copyediting; to Helen Berliner for an inspired index; and to the many members of "sangha-announce" who helped in the Internet search for audiotapes and calligraphies.

When he was working on *Shambhala: The Sacred Path of the Warrior,* the author suggested that we give the manuscript to a number of different readers. He particularly wanted the book read by people untutored in Buddhism or in meditation. In that spirit, in addition to "expert" readers, I also found a number of "naive" people to read the manuscript of *Great Eastern Sun.* I found all the readers very helpful and thank them for offering their candid comments. Thanks to David Swick, Mitchell Levy, Polly Wellenbach, Laura Kurtzman, Johanna Smith, Sue Ozon, Charlotte Keen, Lori Hughes, John Rockwell, Jerry Granelli, and David Burkholder.

Special thanks are due to Mrs. Diana J. Mukpo and to Sakyong Mipham Rinpoche for their contributions to this book. Also, my thanks to Diana Mukpo for her personal encouragement to me and for her continuing support for the editing and publication of her husband's work. Heartfelt thanks to my husband, James Gimian, and my daughter, Jenny Gimian, for being generous and supportive, for giving time and space, friendship, and many smiles. To Jim, special thanks for reading and commenting on the early drafts of the book.

Finally, I would like to offer a song to the Dorje Dradul of Mukpo. Not being a songwriter, I'd like to offer up the words from Laura Smith's heartrending ballad "Duine Air Call," which is a Gaelic phrase, with many interpretations, that was translated for Laura by D. J. MacDonald of Skir Du, Cape Breton, to suggest a soul lost and wandering:

> Duine Air Call Tell me where to now
> I've heard that whisper I know you're near
> You've been coming and going since years ago
> You know how to lead and you know how to follow
> Duine Air Call Oh the tide is high
> There's a new moon waiting for her time to shine
> They've had their moments and I've had mine
> To lead or maybe follow
> All of the distances between you and me
> Between what is and what will be
> All of the changes thinking empty may not fill
> It makes me wonder if faith will ever be enough
> To believe in things I cannot see
> Shadows fall light as feathers on the harbour
> Bouncing off the boat white and the battleship grey
> Do I see the last light of a sun going down
> Or do I see the first light of a brand-new day?
> Shadows fall light as feathers on the harbour
> Someone Somewhere I swear I hear a song
> Sing out loud I am trying to find you Duine Air Call

> Tell me you've just stepped out
> And you won't be gone for long
> Tell me you just stepped out
> And you won't be gone No you won't be gone
> Tell me you won't be gone for long[6]

There is no way in this lifetime or any other to repay the debt of gratitude that I owe to Chögyam Trungpa Rinpoche, Dorje Dradul of Mukpo. I hope that the presentation of the present volume may be a small service to him and that it may rise above the many shortcomings of its editor to proclaim its wisdom. May it benefit beings. May the Great Eastern Sun be victorious.

Dorje Yutri, Carolyn Rose Gimian

May 5, 1998
Trident Mountain House
Tatamagouche, Nova Scotia

---

6. Laura Smith, from her album *B'tween the Earth and My Soul,* ©1994 Cornermuse Productions, Inc. All rights reserved. Used by gracious permission of the artist.

Glossary

The definitions in this glossary are particular to the use of the terms in the text. Unless otherwise designated, foreign terms in the glossary are Sanskrit.

ASHOKA (d. 238? BC)   The last major emperor in the Mauryan dynasty of India. He converted to Buddhism and renounced armed conflict in the eighth year of his reign, when he saw the sufferings that a war he had promoted had inflicted on the conquered people. Buddhism at that time was a small Indian sect, and his patronage of the Buddhist religion is credited with its spread throughout India.

After his conversion, Ashoka resolved to live according to the dharma, to serve his subjects and all humanity. His approach to spreading the dharma was an ecumenical one; he did not try to convert others to the Buddhist faith but instead promoted ethical behavior and the practice of such virtues as honesty, compassion, mercy, nonviolence, and freedom from materialism. He founded hospitals for people and animals and was known for such public works as planting roadside trees, constructing rest houses, and digging wells.

He established a special class of high officials who were designated as "dharma ministers." Their duties were to relieve suffering wherever they encountered it and specifically to look to the special needs of women, neighboring peoples, and other religious communities. He built a number of stupas (religious memorials) and monasteries and inscribed his understanding of the dharma on a number of rocks and pillars, known as the Rock Edicts and the Pillar Edicts. The lion capital of the pillar at Sarnath erected by Ashoka is today the national emblem of India.

BIJA   Dot word, energy, seed, or root power. In a *bija mantra,* or seed syllable, the nature of a particular aspect of reality is concentrated in the form of a symbolic or onomatopoeic sound. In the Shambhala teachings, the author describes the primordial dot as a bija. *See also* mantra *and* om, ah, hum.

BIJA MANTRA   Seed syllable. *See* bija *and* mantra.

BODHISATTVA   Literally, an awake being. A bodhisattva is an individual who has committed himself or herself to helping others and who gives up personal satisfaction for the goal of relieving the suffering of others. In the Buddhist teachings, a bodhisattva is more specifically one who has committed himself or herself to practicing the six paramitas, or the transcendent virtues, of generosity, discipline, patience, exertion, meditation, and knowledge.

BUDDHADHARMA   The teaching of the Buddha or the truth taught by the Buddha. *See also* dharma.

BUDDHA-NATURE   The enlightened basic nature of all beings. In the Shambhala teachings, basic goodness is similar to the concept of buddha-nature. *See also* tathagatagarbha.

CHI   A Chinese term with many meanings, including air, breath, ether, and energy. The concept of chi is not unlike the idea of windhorse in the Shambhala teachings. (See chapter 9, "How to Cultivate the Great Eastern Sun.") The concept of chi is also prevalent in some schools of Japanese philosophy. Chi refers to primordial energy or life force, which may be internal or external—that is, personal or cosmic. Chi as life energy is a central concept in Taoist breathing exercises aimed at strengthening and increasing this energy. *See also* T'ai Chi Ch'uan.

CHUBA   A kind of robe that is a traditional form of dress worn by both men and women in Tibet. There are many varieties of chubas, some made of brocade, others of wool or simple cotton cloth, some fur-lined for warmth.

DHARMA   Truth, norm, phenomenon, or law. Often used to refer to the teachings of the Buddha, which are also called the buddhadharma. Dharma may also refer to the basic manifestation of reality or to the elements of phenomenal existence.

DHARMA ART   A term coined by the author to refer to art that is based on nonaggression and that expresses the basic dharma, or truth, of things as they are.

DRALA In the Shambhala teachings, the manifestation, strength, or bravery that transcends or conquers aggression. Although sometimes conventionally translated as "war god," the author uses *drala* to mean a force or an energy that is above or beyond war.

GARUDA A mythical bird that is half-man and half-beast. The garuda is associated with tremendous speed and power. Like the phoenix, it is said to arise from the ashes of destruction; thus, it has an indestructible quality.

GESAR OF LING A great warrior king in northeast Tibet, the same area from which Chögyam Trungpa hailed. Gesar was a member of the Mukpo clan, to which Trungpa Rinpoche also belonged, and the author felt such a connection with his ancestor that he gave the name Gesar to his third son.

Gesar of Ling's life and exploits inspired the greatest epic of Tibetan literature, which was passed down by oral tradition to the present day. As with many epic heroes, Gesar of Ling's historical origins have been somewhat obscured by his mythic dimension. According to Alexandra David-Neel, who was one of the first Westerners to collect a version of the Gesar epic, he may have lived in the seventh or eighth century AD. Others place him as late as the twelfth century.

In his foreword to Shambhala Publications' edition of *The Superhuman Life of Gesar of Ling* by Alexandra David-Neel and Lama Yongden, Chögyam Trungpa wrote: "[W]e can regard the whole story [of Gesar of Ling] as a display of how the warrior's mind works. Gesar represents the ideal warrior, the principle of all-victorious confidence. As the central force of sanity he conquers all his enemies, the evil forces of the four directions, who turn people's minds away from the true teachings of Buddhism, the teachings that say it is possible to attain ultimate self-realization" (p. 12).

KAGYÜ Tibetan for ear-whispered lineage or the lineage of oral command. *Ka* refers to the oral instructions of the teacher. The Kagyü is one of the four primary lineages of Tibetan Buddhism. The Kagyü teachings were brought from India to Tibet by Marpa the Translator in the eleventh century.

KARMA KAGYÜ *Karma* in Sanskrit means "action" or "deed"; *Kagyü* is Tibetan for the oral or ear-whispered lineage. The Karma Kagyü is a main subdivision of the Kagyü lineage or school of Buddhism, which was founded by Tüsum Khyenpa, the first Karmapa, or head of the Karma Kagyü lineage. Chögyam Trungpa was a major teacher in the Karma Kagyü school of Tibetan Buddhism. *See also* Kagyü.

KARMAPA, HIS HOLINESS THE SIXTEEN GYALWA   The Karmapa is the head of the Karma Kagyü school or lineage of Tibetan Buddhism, to which the author also belonged. *Karmapa* literally means "The Man of Action." *Gyalwa* means "Victorious One." The Karmapa is sometimes also called the Gyalwang Karmapa. *Gyalwang* means "Lord of the Victorious Ones." The sixteenth Karmapa, Rangjung Rigpe Dorje, enthroned the author as the eleventh Trungpa when he was a young child. The Karmapa, like Chögyam Trungpa, escaped from Tibet in 1959. He established his new seat, Rumtek monastery, in Sikkim. He traveled to North America three times, sponsored by Vajradhatu (the author's Buddhist organization) and Karma Triyana Dharmachakra (a Kagyü monastery in upstate New York), in 1974, 1976–77, and 1980. His Holiness passed away from complications of cancer in November 1981.

KHYENTSE RINPOCHE, HIS HOLINESS DILGO   A great teacher of the Nyingma lineage, one of the four major schools of Tibetan Buddhism. Khyentse Rinpoche was one of the important spiritual influences on the author, who first studied with him in Tibet. Later, he hosted Khyentse Rinpoche's visits to North America in 1976 and 1982. In 1982, Khyentse Rinpoche conferred a major Shambhala empowerment, the Sakyong Abhisheka, on the author. His Holiness also conducted the funeral ceremonies for Chögyam Trungpa in 1987. His Holiness remained an adviser to Trungpa Rinpoche's students and community until he himself passed away in 1991.

KYUDO   The traditional art of Japanese archery. The great Japanese archery master Kanjuro Shibata Sensei met and became a close associate of Trungpa Rinpoche in the 1980s. Shibata Sensei has lived part of the year in Boulder, Colorado, since that time and has taught kyudo to many hundreds of the author's Buddhist and Shambhala students.

LAMA   Tibetan for the Sanskrit *guru*, which refers to a realized teacher or spiritual master.

LOHAN   Chinese term for the Sanskrit *arhat*, the ideal of a saint or realized one in the early schools of Buddhism. *Lohan* also refers to a disciple of the Buddha. In some Chinese Buddhist temples and caves, there are impressive statues of the five hundred lohans engaged in various activities or manifesting various states of mind. There is also a group of sixteen or eighteen lohans considered in some forms of Chinese Buddhism to be the major disciples of the Buddha. In the Shambhala teachings, the author used the image of the lohan as the ideal meditator.

MAHAYANA The great vehicle, or the open path. One of the three major traditions of Buddhism. Most of the schools of mahayana Buddhism emphasize the emptiness of phenomena, the development of compassion, and the acknowledgment of universal buddha-nature.

MANTRA Generally, a sacred sound or chant. More specifically, a mantra is a sound or collection of sounds associated with a particular deity or energy in the vajrayana, or tantric, tradition of Buddhism. Mantra is considered to be a form of mind protection, and it was described by the author as onomatopoeic, archetypal, primordial sound.

MARA Literally means death or destroying in both Sanskrit and Pali. In the story of the Buddha's enlightenment, Mara as the embodiment of death attacks the Buddha and tries to prevent him from attaining enlightenment as he is sitting under the bodhi tree meditating just before his final awakening. More generally, the maras refer to the obstacles to enlightenment and the negative forces in the world.

MILAREPA The most famous of all Tibetan poets and one of Tibet's greatest saints. He was the chief disciple of Marpa the Translator who brought the Kagyü teachings from India to Tibet in the eleventh century. After studying with Marpa, Milarepa became a wandering yogin who spent many years in solitary retreat, practicing asceticism and undergoing great deprivation. His beautiful songs of meditative realization have been translated into many Western languages, including an English translation published by Shambhala Publications.

OM, AM, HUM Three of the most famous and most common bija mantras used in visualization and mantra practices in the vajrayana tradition of Tibetan Buddhism. Tibetan deities, which are nontheistic representations of various energies or aspects of reality, are sometimes visualized with the syllables *om, ah,* and *hum* located in the head, throat, and heart centers. This is done as a way of connecting with and actualizing the energies that the deities represent. *See also* bija *and* mantra.

PARINIRVANA   Roughly synonymous with *nirvana, parinirvana* refers to a state of complete liberation, enlightenment, or freedom. Parinirvana is often equated with liberation after death, but it may also refer to liberation during life. It is sometimes used to refer to the death of a monk or nun.

PAWO   Tibetan for warrior. *Pawo* literally means "one who is brave" and is used in the Shambhala teachings to mean one who conquers aggression rather than one who wages war.

PRAJNA   Knowledge, as well as the natural sharpness of awareness, that sees, discriminates, and also cuts through the veils of ignorance.

RIGDEN   The kings of Shambhala, who are said to watch over worldly affairs from their celestial kingdom. Symbolically, the Rigdens represent the complete attainment of bravery and compassion in the Shambhala teachings.

SAMSARA   The vicious cycle of existence, arising from ignorance and characterized by suffering.

SANGHA   The community of Buddhist practitioners. In *Great Eastern Sun,* the author defines *sangha* as follows: "From the Buddhist point of view, friends who create discipline and lighten up our ego are called the *sangha.* In the Shambhala culture, we call such friends *warriors.* Warriors can cheer one another up and together create a warrior society."

SONGTSEN GAMPO   The first great Buddhist king of Tibet. Under his reign, Tibet consolidated a great deal of political power, and in fact, his rule began a period of both political and religious greatness that lasted some two hundred years, from the middle of the seventh century AD until around 836, when Ralpachen, the last of the kings in Songtsen Gampo's line, was assassinated. One of Songtsen Gampo's greatest accomplishments was the introduction of a written Tibetan alphabet, which was required for the translation of Indian Buddhist texts from Sanskrit into Tibetan. He also established the Tibetan capital at Lhasa. He constructed the oldest and most revered temple in Lhasa, the Jokhang, to house a sacred Tibetan statue, the Jobo Rinpoche, which was brought to Tibet by his Chinese wife, a princess of the Chinese court.

In *Born in Tibet,* Chögyam Trungpa's autobiographical account of his upbringing in and departure from Tibet, he talks about encountering sutras carved into the rocks by Songtsen Gampo's ministers while they waited to receive the Chinese princess arriving from China. Trungpa Rinpoche writes: "I returned to Surmang [his monastery] by way of the valley of Bi where in the seventh century King Songtsen-gampo sent his ministers to receive and welcome the Chinese princess he was to marry. Here we saw the Buddhist *sutras* which the ministers had carved on the rocks while waiting for her arrival; some of these are in archaic Tibetan and others in Sanskrit. . . . While the princess was resting in the valley she saw these texts and added a huge image of Vairochana Buddha of over twenty feet in height . . ." (p. 79).

T'AI CHI CH'UAN   A Chinese term that literally means "the supreme ultimate fist." It refers on an outer level to a form of meditation based on physical movements and is also a method of self-defense. T'ai Chi Ch'uan is practiced by performing a sequence of flowing, slowly executed movements, which coordinate mind, body, breath, and spirit and increase the flow of energy, or chi. T'ai Chi Ch'uan is more fundamentally a way of experiencing and harnessing the energies of the universe. It can be described as a warrior discipline and as a means of joining heaven and earth. The origins of T'ai Chi Ch'uan go back to the fourteenth century. *See also* chi.

TANTRA   A synonym for *vajrayana*, one of the three great vehicles, or groups of teachings, within Tibetan Buddhism. *Tantra* literally means "continuity." It may refer to vajrayana texts as well as to the systems of meditation they describe. More generally, it is used by the author to refer to working with or appreciating energy in an enlightened way. *See also* vajrayana.

TATHAGATAGARBHA   *Tathagata* is an epithet of the Buddha, which means "he who has gone beyond." *Garbha* means "womb" or "essence." *Tathagatagarbha* is Sanskrit for buddha-nature, the enlightened basic nature of all beings, which is a central theme of many of the mahayana schools of Buddhism. *See also* buddha-nature.

VAJRA (TIB. *dorje*)   Adamantine, or having the qualities of a diamond. *Vajra* refers to the basic indestructible nature of wisdom and enlightenment.

VAJRA SANGHA   The community of vajrayana Buddhist practitioners.

VAJRAYANA   The diamond way or the indestructible vehicle. Vajrayana is the third of the three great yanas, or groups of teachings, within

Tibetan Buddhism. It is synonymous with *tantra.* The lineage of Tibetan Buddhism to which the author belonged, the Karma Kagyü, was one of the major vajrayana, or tantric, lineages of Buddhist teachings in Tibet.

YANA A vehicle, in which, symbolically, the practitioner travels on the road to enlightenment. The different vehicles, or yanas, correspond to different views of the journey, and each yana comprises a body of knowledge and practice. The three great yanas in Tibetan Buddhism are the hinayana, mahayana, and vajrayana. *See also* mahayana *and* vajrayana.

YOGA Literally, yoke or union. Although commonly associated these days with several systems of physical postures and exercise, yoga has a much more spiritual aspect. In Hinduism, yoga has the sense of harnessing or yoking oneself to God and seeking union with the divine. In the tantric Buddhist tradition, yoga is a means of synchronizing body and mind to discover reality or truth. Great tantric practitioners like Milarepa are considered part of the yogic tradition in Tibet.

YOGIN A practitioner of yoga or one dedicated to the yogic tradition. *Yogin* is non-gender-specific. A male practitioner of yoga is a yogi; a female practitioner is a yogini.

ZABUTON A rectangular meditation mat, usually about 2 feet by 3 feet, that is placed under a zafu or gomden for meditation practice. *See also* zafu.

ZAFU A fluffy, round meditation cushion, usually stuffed with kapok, developed in the Zen Buddhist practice of meditation. The author originally recommended the use of the zafu by his Buddhist and Shambhala students but later replaced it with a rectangular foam-filled meditation cushion of his own design, the *gomden.*

Sources

What follows is a list of the sources for prose and poetry, including dates and locations of the talks on which the chapters are based.

To Gesar of Ling
> Composed July 4, 1975. Translated from the Tibetan by the author and David Rome.
> Reprinted from *First Thought Best Thought: One Hundred and Eight Poems,* by Chögyam Trungpa, p. 87.

Prologue: The Kingdom, the Cocoon, the Great Eastern Sun
> SOURCE: Public talk, Boston, Massachusetts, March 27, 1980.

PART ONE: PROFOUND

PRIMORDIAL STROKE

1. A Dot in the Open Sky
> SOURCE: Level Five, Talk One, Boulder, Colorado, November 16, 1979.

1111 Pearl Street: Off Beat
> Composed June 1976.
> Originally published in *First Thought Best Thought: One Hundred and Eight Poems,* by Chögyam Trungpa, p. 108. Reprinted here from *Timely Rain: Selected Poetry of Chögyam Trungpa,* p. 123.

2. Working with Early Morning Depression
> SOURCE: Level Five, Talk Two, Boulder, Colorado, November 17, 1979.

3. Overcoming Physical Materialism
> SOURCE: Level Five, Talk Three, Boulder, Colorado, November 18, 1979.

THE PRIMORDIAL DOT

4. The Cosmic Sneeze
   SOURCE: Level Five, Talk One, Boston, Massachusetts, March 28, 1980.
5. Discipline in the Four Seasons
   SOURCE: Level Five, Talk Two, Boston, Massachusetts, March 29, 1980.
6. Mirrorlike Wisdom
   SOURCE: Level Five, Talk Three, Boston, Massachusetts, March 30, 1980.

Good Morning within the Good Morning
   Composed March 30, 1980.
   Reprinted from *Warrior Songs,* by Chögyam Trungpa (Halifax, Nova Scotia: Trident Publications, 1991). Used by permission.

PART TWO: BRILLIANT

SACRED EXISTENCE: JOINING HEAVEN AND EARTH

7. Sacredness: Natural Law and Order
   SOURCE: Level Five, Talk One, Boulder, Colorado, October 30, 1980.
8. The King of Basic Goodness
   SOURCE: Level Five, Talk Two, Boulder, Colorado, October 31, 1980.
9. How to Cultivate the Great Eastern Sun
   SOURCE: Level Five, Talk Three, Boulder, Colorado, November 1, 1980.

PART THREE: JUST

THE PASSION TO BE

10. Blamelessness: How to Love Yourself
    SOURCE: Level Five, Talk One, Boulder, Colorado, January 8, 1982.

Four Untitled Poems
    From an unpublished Tibetan manuscript, January 8, 1982.
    Translated by the Nalanda Translation Committee.

11. Attaining the Higher Realms
    SOURCE: Level Five, Talk Two, Boulder, Colorado, January 9,
    1982.
12. The Big No
    SOURCE: Level Five, Talk Three, Boulder, Colorado, January 10,
    1982.
How to Know No
    Composed January 1, 1980.
    Originally published in *First Thought Best Thought: One Hundred
    and Eight Poems*, by Chögyam Trungpa, pp. 167–68.

FEARLESS RELAXATION

13. Aloneness and the Seven Virtues of the Higher Realms
    SOURCE: Level Five, Talk Two, New York City, January 23, 1982.
The Meek: Powerfully Nonchalant and Dangerously Self-Satisfying
    Composed: May 13, 1983.
    Originally published in *First Thought Best Thought: One Hundred
    and Eight Poems*, by Chögyam Trungpa. Reprinted from *Timely
    Rain: Selected Poetry of Chögyam Trungpa*, pp. 165–66.
14. The King of the Four Seasons
    SOURCE: Level Five, Talk Three, New York City, January 24, 1982.
Seasoning Life
    Unpublished poem, composed May 9, 1983.

PART FOUR: POWERFUL

THE WARRIOR'S CRY

15. The Basic Gasp of Goodness
    SOURCE: Level Five, Talk One, Berkeley, California, April 23,
    1982.
16. Helping Others
    SOURCE: Level Five, Talk Two, Berkeley, California, April 24,
    1982.
Sanity Is Joyful
    Composed October 27, 1982.
    Reprinted from *Warrior Songs*, by Chögyam Trungpa (Halifax,
    Nova Scotia: Trident Publications, 1991). Used by permission.

17. Transmission
> SOURCE: Level Five, Talk Three, Berkeley, California, April 25, 1982.

Anthem
> Composed 1977. Translated from the Tibetan by the author and others. Used by permission of the Nalanda Translation Committee.

PART FIVE: ALL-VICTORIOUS

THE WARRIOR'S SMILE

18. A Question of Heart
> SOURCE: Public talk, Vancouver, British Columbia, July 29, 1982.

19. The Mukpo Clan
> SOURCE: Level Five, Talk One, Vancouver, British Columbia, July 30, 1982.

Auspicious Coincidence: Wealth and Vision
> Composed February 24, 1980.
> Reprinted from *Warrior Songs*, by Chögyam Trungpa (Halifax, Nova Scotia: Trident Publications, 1991). Used by permission.

Excerpt from a longer poem entitled "Haiku"
> Composed April 25, 1980.
> Reprinted from *Warrior Songs*, by Chögyam Trungpa (Halifax, Nova Scotia: Trident Publications, 1991). Used by permission.

20. Beyond Depression
> SOURCE: Level Five, Talk Two, Vancouver, British Columbia, July 31, 1982.

Battle Cry
> Composed September 5, 1982.
> Reprinted from *Warrior Songs*, by Chögyam Trungpa (Halifax, Nova Scotia: Trident Publications, 1991). Used by permission.

21. The Great Eastern Sun: The Dot in Space
> SOURCE: Level Five, Talk Three, Vancouver, British Columbia, August 1, 1982.

Closing Dedication
> EXCERPT FROM *Lightning of Blessings: Supplication to the Imperial Warriors,* by Chögyam Trungpa. Composed 1981. Translated from the Tibetan by the Nalanda Translation Committee.

Author's Notes

This section includes the author's notes for the talks on which this book is based, translated from the author's Tibetan note cards by the Nalanda Translation Committee, with special thanks to John Rockwell. Notes for the other sources could not be located.

PRIMORDIAL STROKE

1. A Dot in the Open Sky

trust	basic goodness
renunciation	setting sun (hierarchy)
letting go/daring	loving toward others (independent)

2. Working with Early Morning Depression

Renunciation of habitual patterns: joy of basic goodness/sadness of the setting sun

Then, Ashé arises, and you are certain what needs to be accepted and rejected.

Therefore, you have love for your teacher and respect for your elders: hierarchy.

3. Overcoming Physical Materialism

Letting go:	Because you have no fear of ignorance, you are friendly to yourself. Therefore, you are always friendly to others (independent).
Wisdom:	You attain wisdom and conviction in hierarchy.
Because of:	discipline of body, truth in speech, mind without deception, there arises a king who joins heaven and earth.

Sacred Existence: Joining Heaven and Earth

7. Sacredness: Natural Law and Order

Basic goodness

Trust   Patience brings healthiness.
         Freedom from laziness brings exertion.
         Faith brings fearlessness.

8. The King of Basic Goodness

Revulsion arises from meditation.
   1. Caring for others (free from doubt) brings daring.
   2. Knowing what to accept and reject brings gentleness.
   3. Because there is a king who joins heaven and earth, body and mind are synchronized.

9. How to Cultivate the Great Eastern Sun

Letting go   mindfulness, awareness, decency
              windhorse, seeing basic goodness, genuine heart
              sadness and joy, Great Eastern Sun

                   Radiating confidence, peaceful,
                   Illuminating discipline
                   Ruler of the three worlds

The Passion to Be

10. Blamelessness: How to Love Yourself

benefiting others   revulsion

trust   warrior

healthiness, head and shoulders, and joy

not blaming anyone

11. Attaining the Higher Realms

Daring: Being free, one is gentle to oneself and loving to others.

           Therefore, one constantly delights in compassion, enjoying the world and its inhabitants.

           Through a dot in space,

one learns how to eat, walk, sleep, and sit.
This gives rise to the higher realms.

12. The Big No

Decency: Not regarding yourself as better and criticizing others. (joy)

Able to trust.

Because one is free from trickery, one is free from hope and fear.

FEARLESS RELAXATION

13. Aloneness and the Seven Virtues of the Higher Realms

sadness aloneness   tenderness to oneself (devotion)
love for others

From this, a dot in space, understanding the four behaviors.[1]

This gives rise to the seven virtues of the higher realms: (1) faith, (2) discipline, (3) daring, (4) learning, (5) decorum, (6) modesty, (7) discriminating awareness.

14. The King of the Four Seasons

From a dot in space arising,
there is no setting-sun view. Decorum.

Therefore, one achieves fearlessness (like a tiger).

Fearlessness brings looseness.

This gives rise to natural hierarchy,
and in that looseness free of fear,
delight arises from the start.

---

1. These are probably eating, walking, lying down, and sitting.

Resources

For information regarding the Shambhala Training program, please contact:

Shambhala Training International
1084 Tower Road
Halifax, Nova Scotia
Canada B3H 2Y5

Phone: (902) 425-4275, ext. 27
E-mail: kikisoso@shambhala.org
Web site: *www.shambhala.org*. The Web site contains information about the more than 100 centers affiliated with Shambhala.

For Europe, please contact:

Shambhala Europe
Wilhelmstrasse 20
D35037 Marburg, Germany

Phone: 49 6421 17020
E-mail: *europe@shambhala.org*

For audio- and videotape recordings of lectures and seminars by the author, please contact:

Kalapa Recordings
1084 Tower Road
Halifax, Nova Scotia
Canada B3H 2Y5

Phone: (902) 420-1118, ext. 19
E-mail: *recordings@shambhala.org*
Web site: *www.shambhala.org/recordings*

For information about the archive of the author's work—which includes more than 5,000 audio recordings, 1,000 video recordings, original Tibetan manuscripts, correspondence, and more than 30,000 photographs—please contact:

The Shambhala Archives
1084 Tower Road
Halifax, Nova Scotia
Canada B3H 2Y5

Phone: (902) 425-4275, ext. 21
Web site: *www.shambhala.org/archives*

The Naropa Institute is the only accredited, Buddhist-inspired university in North America. It offers an undergraduate degree and graduate programs in a variety of disciplines. For more information, contact:

The Naropa Institute
2130 Arapahoe Avenue
Boulder, Colorado 80302
(303) 444-0202
Web site: *www.naropa.edu*

Books by Chögyam Trungpa

*The Art of Calligraphy: Joining Heaven and Earth
*Born in Tibet
*Cutting Through Spiritual Materialism
*Dharma Art
**The Essential Chögyam Trungpa
*The Heart of the Buddha
 Illusion's Game: The Life and Teaching of Naropa
 The Life of Marpa the Translator (translated by the Nalanda Translation Committee under the direction of Chögyam Trungpa)
 The Lion's Roar
**Meditation in Action
**The Myth of Freedom and the Way of Meditation
 Orderly Chaos: The Mandala Principle
**The Path Is the Goal: A Basic Handbook of Buddhist Meditation
 The Rain of Wisdom: The Essence of the Ocean of True Meaning (translated by the Nalanda Translation Committee under the direction of Chögyam Trungpa)
**Shambhala: The Sacred Path of the Warrior
*The Tibetan Book of the Dead: The Great Liberation through Hearing in the Bardo (translated with commentary by Francesca Fremantle and Chögyam Trungpa)
*Timely Rain: Selected Poetry of Chögyam Trungpa
*Training the Mind and Cultivating Loving-Kindness
 Transcending Madness: The Experience of the Six Bardos

* indicates that the title is a good introductory treatment of the subject matter. Other titles are more specialized.

** indicates that the title is particularly suited for readers newly interested in meditation, the Shambhala training, and Buddhism.

Index

ཉི་ཟླ་བདུད་ཀྱི་གཡུལ་ལས་ཊག་ཏུ་རྒྱལ།

བདག་ཏུ་འཛིན་པའི་ཞེ་ཚོམ་གྲོལ་ནས་ཀྱང་།

བོང་མ་དཔའ་བོ་རྣམས་ཀྱི་མཇོད་པ་བཞིན།

བདག་ཀྱང་ཁྱེད་ཀྱི་རྗེས་སུ་འཇུག་ནས་ཀྱང་།

ཁམས་གསུམ་འགྲོ་བའི་སྤུག་བསྒལ་བསལ་བ་དང་།

ཛྙོགས་སྨན་གསར་པའི་བདེ་སྐྱིད་བཟང་པོ་ཡི།

ཤར་ཆེན་ཉི་མ་ཁམ་རྩལ་ཡི་དཔལ།

ཐོག་མེད་མྱུར་དུ་འབྱུབ་པར་བྱིན་གྱིས་རྫོབས།

May we be ever victorious over the warring evils
of the setting sun.
May ego fixation and hesitation be liberated.
Emulating your actions, imperial warriors,
May we follow in your footsteps.
Grant your blessings so that the suffering of beings
in the three realms may be dispelled
And so that the excellent peace and happiness of
the new golden age,
The Great Eastern Sun, the glory of Shambhala,
May be realized quickly without obstruction.

Shambhala Dragon Editions

The Art of War, by Sun Tzu. Translated by Thomas Cleary.

The Awakened One: A Life of the Buddha, by Sherab Chödzin Kohn.

The Awakening of Zen, by D. T. Suzuki.

Bodhisattva of Compassion: The Mystical Tradition of Kuan Yin, by John Blofeld.

The Buddhist I-Ching. Translated by Thomas Cleary.

The Compass of Zen, by Zen Master Seung Sahn. Foreword by Stephen Mitchell.

Cutting Through Spiritual Materialism, by Chögyam Trungpa.

The Diamond Sutra and The Sutra of Hui-neng. Translated by A. F. Price and Wong Mou-lam. Forewords by W. Y. Evans-Wentz and Christmas Humphreys.

The Essence of Buddhism: An Introduction to Its Philosophy and Practice, by Traleg Kyabgon.

The Experience of Insight: A Simple and Direct Guide to Buddhist Meditation, by Joseph Goldstein.

A Flash of Lightning in the Dark of Night: A Guide to the Bodhisattva's Way of Life, by Tenzin Gyatso, the Fourteenth Dalai Lama.

Glimpses of Abhidharma, by Chögyam Trungpa.

Great Eastern Sun: The Wisdom of Shambhala, by Chögyam Trungpa.

Insight Meditation: The Practice of Freedom, by Joseph Goldstein.

Lieh-tzu: A Taoist Guide to Practical Living, by Eva Wong.

Living with Kundalini: The Autobiography of Gopi Krishna, by Gopi Krishna.

The Lotus-Born: The Life Story of Padmasambhava, by Yeshe Tsogyal. Translated by Erik Pema Kunsang.

Mastering the Art of War, by Zhuge Liang and Liu Ji. Translated and edited by Thomas Cleary.

The Mysticism of Sound and Music, by Hazrat Inayat Khan.

The Myth of Freedom and the Way of Meditation, by Chögyam Trungpa.

Nine-Headed Dragon River: Zen Journals 1969-1982, by Peter Matthiessen.

Returning to Silence: Zen Practice in Daily Life, by Dainin Katagiri. Foreword by Robert Thurman.

Rumi's World: The Life and Work of the Great Sufi Poet, by Annemarie Schimmel.

Shambhala: The Sacred Path of the Warrior, by Chögyam Trungpa.

The Shambhala Dictionary of Buddhism and Zen. Translated by Michael H. Kohn.

The Spiritual Teaching of Ramana Maharshi, by Ramana Maharshi. Foreword by C. G. Jung.

Start Where You Are: A Guide to Compassionate Living, by Pema Chödrön.

The Sutra of Hui-neng, Grand Master of Zen: With Hui-neng's Commentary on the Diamond Sutra. Translated by Thomas Cleary.

Tao Teh Ching, by Lao Tzu. Translated by John C. H. Wu.

Teachings of the Buddha, revised and expanded edition. Edited by Jack Kornfield.

Vitality, Energy, Spirit: A Taoist Sourcebook. Translated and edited by Thomas Cleary.

The Way of the Bodhisattva: A Translation of the Bodhicharyāvatāra. Translated by the Padmakara Translation Group.

Wen-tzu: Understanding the Mysteries, by Lao-tzu. Translated by Thomas Cleary.

Zen Essence: The Science of Freedom. Translated and edited by Thomas Cleary.